POLICY SCIENCE

Effective Policy Making
under the Age of Turbulence

Gi-Heon Kwon, Ph.D

PARKYOUNG
publishing&company

POLICY SCIENCE:
EFFECTIVE POLICY MAKING &
SMART POLICY FRAMEWORK 4.0

The unfolding of the 21st century has brought the world into a new and different turn. It's an era of time, speed, and uncertainty. The 4th Industrial revolution is characterized by volatility, uncertainty, complexity, ambiguity. Under is these times of turbulence, innovation is crucial to achieve the transformation of governance under the society 4.0. To achieve innovation and transformation, effective policymaking is indispensable.

As the 21st century unfolds, we are living in a chaotic and turbulent society. Speed of thought becomes very important as information and knowledge is the most critical factor of national competitiveness. To achieve national competitiveness, thereby building a great and strong nation, effective policymaking is crucial to achieve government innovation and national transformation.

Such swirl of information revolution requires an unsullied evaluation of the existing governance model and its operating system. In particular, up until now, the bureaucratic model has led the modern development and its operating system is largely dependent on the steep, rigid, and hierarchical system based on command and control.

But it's not true in this knowledge society anymore. Ordinary people can access information and knowledge easily; they sometimes know important information before the government. The red-zone disappears; there is no secret. Power shifts. As a result, modern society becomes transparent at an increasing speed. The cooperative or network governance based on e-Governance, in which government consults with its partners, the corporate business, and NGOs in the civil society, with the spirit of trust and collaboration, becomes a more and more effective form of governance in this modern knowledge society, even in the developing countries.

The full integration of knowledge and skills stacked in thousands of years can be attributed to digitization or advancement of information and communication technology(ICT). The concept of time and space was totally obliterated due to the innovation of broadcasting and communication.

How these kinds of enormous change and innovation, swirling from the high-technological environmental changes such as the SMART revolution and the INDUSTRIAL revolution, will impact the academic discipline of policy science, effective policy-making specifically? What should be the new theoretical principle and philosophy of policy science to break-away the so-called criticism of the *impoverished professionalism*' facing the science of public administration? And how could we then academically link the theoretical principles of the knowledge-created Smart e-Government with the traditional Policy Science?

This book is written as an attempt to answer these kinds of academic as well as practical questions, searching for a new paradigm of the policy framework to presenting the most appropriate strategy facing the developing countries in this 21st century.

The author uses the theories from the field of public policy, public administration, new public management, and new governance to explain the paradigm of effective policymaking. In short, this book is about the theories and praxis of effective policymaking, especially in developing countries.

Every year a large number of government officials in the developing countries apply for the Global MPA e-Government& Local Innovation Program, the Graduate School of Governance, SKKU, the graduate institution the author is associated, indicates that Korean e-Government and Smart policy framework has a real reputation to be benchmarked from the perspective of developing countries.

The Korean model is really attractive for them, especially because this country has developed its model up to the world best within a few decades, especially from the Korean War-torn ashes of 1953. The country, then receiving ODAs from the then advanced nations, now accomplished the world's best model and become one of the OECD nations to offer the ODAs to many developing countries. Hence, the lessons from this country, who developed with her own will& commitment, leadership, and policy strategies, would be more plausible and appropriate for the other fellow developing countries who also ardently want to transform their nations to the world-best at this moment.

On a personal note, I owe a profound debt to the dozens of people who have contributed in one way or another to this book. To name their contributions would fill another volume like the size of this one, so I must leave much unsaid. Nevertheless, I must acknowledge the particular contributions of a few people.

I owe my greatest thanks to the CEO of Tadafur Information Technology, Mr. Adil Kassabi who has been a constant source of insight and inspiration. Building upon many conversations and exchanges of our vision and thoughts, we envisioned an ambitious enterprise of setting up a globally leading academic program on effective policy science and digital transformation especially centering on the Middle East and North Africa. This monograph, "POLICY SCIENCE: Effective Policy Making and Smart Policy Framework 4.0" is an academic result of those exchanged thought and reflections.

I would also like to express my gratitude to the Global MPA students at the graduate school of Governance, SKKU in Korea. The SKKU, the institution that I associated, has been operating Global MPA Program in which 20 mid-career officials all around the world came to learn e-Government, Policy Science, and Innovation theories & Praxis of Korea. This book was written to introduce the Policy Science and Smart Governance of Korea when offering those GMPA classes.

With this backdrop, I have discussed this project and received much valuable feedback from the GMPA students. To name a few, I would like to give my special thanks to the GMPA Coordinator Dasol Lee, Mr. Bayoumi Ahmed Bayoumi Nagyeb, a GMPA student from Egypt, Mr. Reginald Ugaddan currently a professor at the University of Philippine, Once Ph.D. student and a GMPA Lecturer at SKKU, and other GMPA students who gave extremely valuable comments and feedback on this book. Also, they have been a great source of strength and inspiration to me during my writings on this monograph. Again, I would like to give my special thanks to them.

April 2021

Gi-Heon Kwon, Ph.D

Professor of Public Policy & E-Government

Director of Global e-Policy & e-Government Institute,

Graduate School of Governance,

SKKU-Samsung Foundation

Table of Contents

PART 2 POLICY PARADIGM & MODELS

PART 3   POLICY ANALYSIS & IMPLEMENTATION

PART 4   THE 4TH INDUSTRIAL REVOLUTION

PART 1

POLICY DESIGN:
EFFECTIVE POLICY MAKING AND SMART POLICY FRAMEWORK

Chapter 1

EFFECTIVE POLICY MAKING
The Fundamental Theory for Effective Policy Making

When paradigm changes, the world itself changes.

Thomas Kuhn

 **>>> Objectives**

The purpose of this chapter is to elucidate the paradigm of effective policy making. This chapter focuses on the theoretical foundation of effective policy making by revisiting the Lasswell paradigm of policy science.

First, it will review the Lasswell paradigm of policy science.

Second, it will highlight to give a holistic understanding of effective policy making and its relationship with new governance, national innovation, and human dignity,

Third, it will reexamine the important notion of a strong and great nation–it's definition, dimensions, and policy criteria to realize the vision of a strong and great nation.

Finally, it will elucidate the critical methodology of effective policy making, including new capacity building, comprehensive design, and its implication with the policy case of the COVID-19 crisis.

Lasswell Paradigm of Policy Science

As the 21st century unfolds, we find ourselves living in a chaotic society in the grip of the COVID-19 pandemic. Simultaneously, we are also undergoing the 4th Industrial revolution, characterized by volatility, uncertainty, complexity, and ambiguity. Under these turbulent circumstances, innovation is crucial to the transformation of governance within the concept of society 4.0. To achieve such innovation and transformation, an effective policy framework is indispensable. As evidenced by the COVID-19 crisis response, smart governance based on an effective policy framework could save thousands of lives. As the Korean cases demonstrate, agile governance with an effective policy framework was answer. By utilizing big data and evidence-based scientific analyses, which can lead to effective policy making and implementation, we can reach for a brighter and more creative future as a nation.

This book is about the theories and practices ("praxis") of effective policy making. To shed light on the new paradigm of effective policy making, we need to briefly revisit the Lasswell paradigm of Policy Science as H. Lasswell was the founder of Policy Science.

The modern policy science, called policy science of democracy by Harold Lasswell, initiated by H. Lasswell (1951) in his article, "The Policy Orientation." He argued that policy science should study the systemic order of fundamental problems, for example, civilization clash, social conflict and change, and world revolution and war. By suggesting problem orientation, contextual orientation, and interdisciplinary orientation, he highlighted that the policy science of democracy should pursue human dignity. For this vision, each government should complete its policy orientation by researching the policy process (of) as well as policy content (in).

Figure 1-1   Modern Theory of Lasswell Paradigm

Purpose of Policy Science

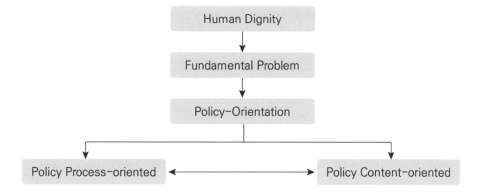

> Lasswell,
> The Policy Orientation(1951)

* Policy science is a study taking place at the level of systemic order in order to faithfully realize human dignity.
* Civilization clash, Contemporary change, World revolution, and Systemic-order Problems.
* Problem-oriented, Context-oriented, Interdisciplinary Study

Human Dignity
↓
Fundamental Problem
↓
Policy-Orientation

Policy Process-oriented ←→ Policy Content-oriented

The Paradigm of Effective Policy Making

1. Effective Policy Making and New Governance

As the 21st century unfolds, we are living in a chaotic and turbulent society, characterized by time, speed, and uncertainty. Speed of thought becomes very important as information and knowledge is the most critical factor of national competitiveness. To achieve national competitiveness, thereby building a great and strong nation, effective policy making is indispensable to achieve government innovation and national transformation.

Such swirl of information revolution requires an unsullied evaluation of the existing governance model and its operating system. In particular, up until now, the bureaucratic model has led the modern development and its operating system is largely dependent on the steep, rigid, and hierarchical system based on command and control.

But it's not true in this knowledge society anymore. Ordinary people can access information and knowledge easily; they sometimes know important information before the government. The red-zone disappears; there is no secret. Power shifts. As a result, modern society becomes transparent at an increasing speed. The cooperative or network governance based on e-Governance, in which government consults with its partners – i.e., corporate business, and NGOs in the civil society – with the spirit of trust and collaboration, becomes a more and more effective form of governance in this modern knowledge society, even in the developing countries.

The figure below shows the vision and direction of new governance. It also shows globalization, innovation, and leadership challenges that global leaders should face in the turbulence of the 4th industrial revolution. Digital is characterized by time, speed, and uncertainty. Therefore, in this turbulent modern age, speed of thought, and a new direction of innovation is critical, and that is effective policy making should be targeting.

Figure 1-2 Globalization, Innovation & Leadership Challenges In the Turbulence of 4th Industrial Revolution

2. Effective Policy Making and National Innovation

For the most developing nation, the dream of national innovation is to achieve a great and strong nation. This dream and vision start with effective policy making. A great nation should be built upon the effective policy making and strong foundation of the governance system in which government, business, and civil society are most effectively functioned in society.

Effective policy making starts with the theoretical foundation of understanding two critical features of public policy: rational aspect and political aspect. To enhance the rational aspects of public policy, knowledge management and performance management are critical, while incorporating the political aspects, conflict management is inevitable. For the former, we need innovation and foresight approach, while for the latter we need a new governance approach as new governance emphasizes the horizontal network based on the spirit of trust and collaboration.

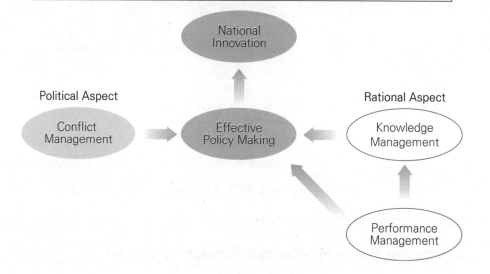

Figure 1-3 Effective Policy Making(1)

- National innovation will be realized by Effective policy making.
- Effective policy making will create Smart e-government system in which government-business-civil society will be most-effectively functioned in your society.

3. Effective Policy Making and Human Dignity

H. Lasswell(1951) argued that the supreme vision of policy science should be human dignity.

For the developing nations, this vision can be expressed as a strong and great national building: maybe the strong first and then to become a great nation. Human dignity is too much philosophical terminology and seems to be far away, so we need more practical goals such as to become a strong and great nation.

What is strong and what is great, then? 'The great' means beyond 'the strong.' To be strong is only the necessary condition for the great nation but not sufficient. The great nation needs more. For example, the great nation should provide the peaceful community and foundation in which freedom and justice flow like a great river so that each citizen loves each other with full trust and respect, and could pursue his or her well-being and self-realization with his own free will and wisdom. Also, internationally the great nation should be willing to share its resources and technologies with its neighborhood or the other less-developed countries to make this world for the better place such that people could live in a genuinely peaceful, co-existent, and co-prosperous environment.

To become a strong and great nation, the governments, especially in the developing areas, need a new capacity building to enhance the government officials' capacity for effective policy making.

For this purpose, some key agenda of the capacity building should be:

1) Identify "fundamental problems" faced in your society.
2) Perform evidence-based policy analysis and policy making
3) Also, learn the foundation of policy science with Smart e-Government, e-Transformation, and Attitude change for the behavioral perspectives.

Figure 1-4   Effective Policy Making & Online Training

What is Human dignity and What will be learned for Effective Policy Making?

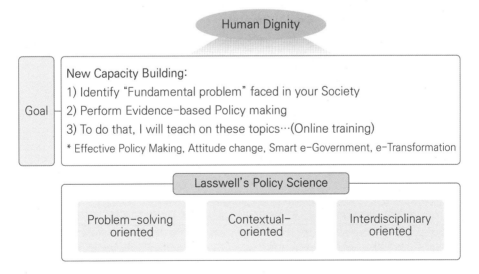

4. Strong and Great Nation: Dimension

Let's elaborate on the concept of a strong and great nation in a more detailed fashion. What are the dimensions required to become a strong and great nation?

There are five capitals that a nation needs to build up in this creative knowledge society. They are economic and physical capital, human capital, social capital, positive psychology capital, and spiritual capital. It shows a national developmental stage. To become a strong nation, it needs a strong foundation of economic, defense, and human capital. Also, it needs a strong infrastructure such as physical roads, highways, transportation, and smart ICT infrastructures. In other words, a strong nation has a strong foundation of physical, economic, and human capital. These are visible capitals.

Figure 1-5 Strong & Great Nation: Five Capitals

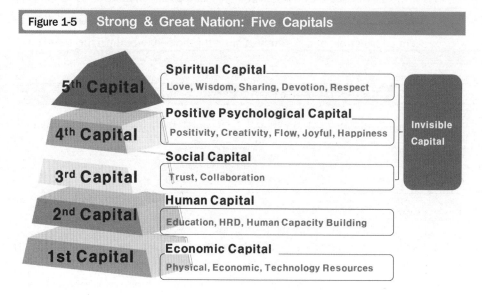

* Base on the theory of positive psychology of M. Seligman and C. Mihalyi

To become a great nation, however, it needs more. We do not automatically consider a nation, even if strong, as a great nation. A great nation is not only strong but needs invisible capitals that is, social, positive psychological, and spiritual capitals. Especially in the age of creative knowledge, these invisible capitals become more valuable. Trust building, cooperative attitudes, positive citizen with creativity, love, and wise nation sharing its wisdom or wealth with other countries, this hidden capital will become more noble and valuable especially in the uncertain and turbulent age of the 4th Industrial revolution.

5. Strong and Great Nation: Policy Criteria

What would be the policy criteria that a strong and great nation should follow? In the same vein, what are the most critical criteria of good governance? The policy criteria for good governance are composed of efficiency, democracy, and reflexivity.

Figure 1-6	Effective Policy Making(2)

- Effective policy making promotes the three dimensions: Efficiency, Democracy and Reflexivity.

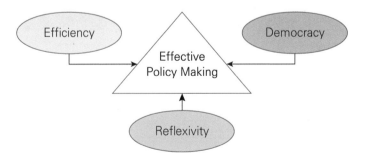

Efficiency. The strong and great nation should be strong and efficient. It should perform effective policy making. From the standpoint of smart e-Government, efficiency dimension has four elements: 1) One and any stop portal government, 2) Paperless and building-less government with cost reduction, 3) clean and transparent government with zero corruption, 4) digital government with knowledge management.

Democracy. The strong and great nation embraces democratic values. From the political and process standpoint, democracy is valuable and indispensable. It indicates not only political participation through election or voting but also participation in the policy making employing features of digital government. Hence, democracy dimension has two critical elements: 1) e-Policy with digital participation in the policy process, 2) e-Politics with digital voting, digital congress, and digital legislation.

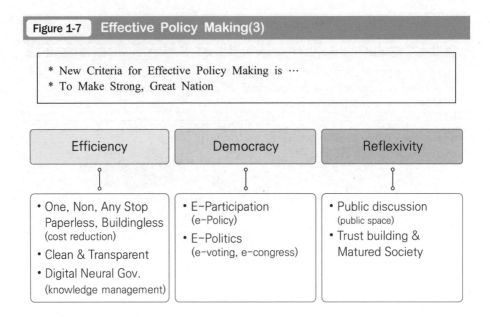

Figure 1-7 Effective Policy Making(3)

* New Criteria for Effective Policy Making is ⋯
* To Make Strong, Great Nation

Efficiency	Democracy	Reflexivity

• One, Non, Any Stop
  Paperless, Buildingless
  (cost reduction)
• Clean & Transparent
• Digital Neural Gov.
  (knowledge management)
	• E−Participation
	  (e−Policy)
	• E−Politics
	  (e−voting, e−congress)
		• Public discussion
		  (public space)
		• Trust building &
		  Matured Society

Reflexivity. The strong and great nation is reflexive. Reflexivity is a philosophical term. It refers to a supreme vision that a nation-state could realize. For instance, it means a society in which human dignity will be strictly observed; therefore, the individual citizen could freely actualize self-esteem and self-realization. In a nutshell, it is a trustful and mature society in which citizens can freely discuss social issues or public agenda using the public space in the smart e-Government. It is the highest dimension of effective policy making.

Let's discuss this important issue from another angle. The figure below displays the policy design that a strong and great nation should follow. To put it another way, it shows the great vision that national innovation should attain. It indicates dimension, institution, method, and model. From the dimension perspective, it shows efficiency, democracy, and reflexivity. From the institution perspective, it is an economic method, political system, and philosophical vision respectively. The vision can be expressed as BAR society, it means, Spiritually beautiful, Materially affluent, and Humanely rewarding society. And this vision

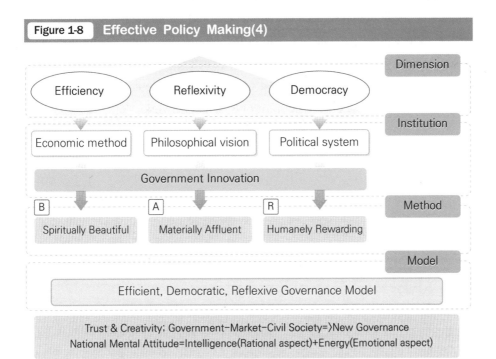

Figure 1-8   Effective Policy Making(4)

can be fulfilled by the efficient, democratic, and reflexive governance model in which effective policy making should pursue to make a trustful and creative society. Also, this vision can be realized when the three critical actors, government-market-civil society, will be harmoniously collaborating with the spirit of trust and network. Then, the vision of a strong and great nation will be accomplished in which citizens can fully express their creativity and collective intelligence with positive, loving, and gratitude attitudes.

6. Effective Policy Making: New Capacity Building

To achieve the vision of a strong and great nation, mentioned above, we need a new capacity building for effective policy making. The following figure shows its new paradigm. It consists of the supreme value of human dignity, intermediate goal, research, and action orientation. The realization of human dignity is the vision of a strong and great nation. To achieve this vision, the government should upgrade policy capacity, management capacity, and infrastructure capacity. Also, by upgrading the research capacity of policy analysis, including quantitative and qualitative methodologies, each government should formulate the action plan and road map to achieve its goal and vision. At the right side of the figure, it shows a desirable new governance principle and its structures. In other words, effective policy making could be accomplished when the government, business, and civil society could collaborate with the spirit of trust and network.

Figure 1-9 New Paradigm of Policy Science

New Capacity Building: Effective Policy Making

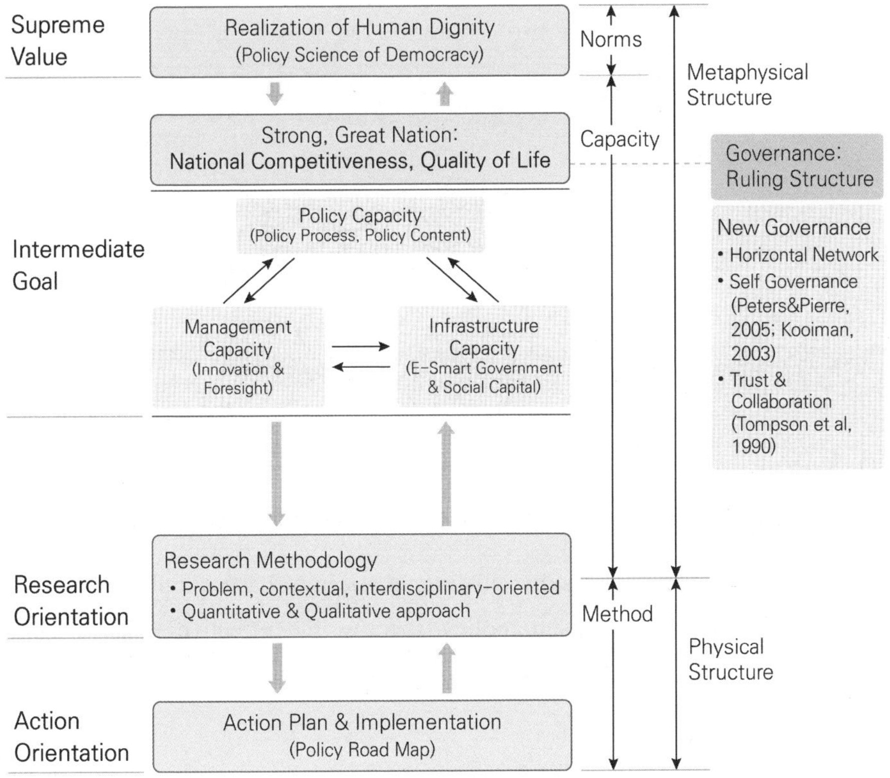

7. Effective Policy Making: Micro and Macro Meaning

Effective policy making, in this book, is defined following two perspectives: micro and macro. The micro perspective of effective policy making denotes specifically to theory and methods for effective decision making. On the other hand, macro perspective is used as the theory and methods of the overall policy processes. In particular, a typical policy process includes agenda setting, policy making, implementation, and evaluation. Employing the macro perspective of effective policy making requires the adoption of proper theory and method.

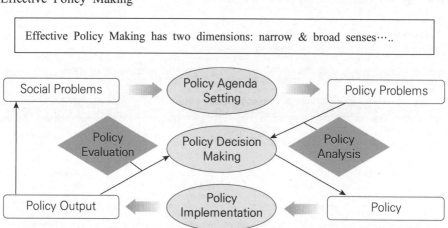

Figure 1-10 Policy Science

8. Effective Policy Making: Check Points for Quality Control

For an effective policy making government need to have a tool-kit for policy quality management. To ensure policy success, the effective policy making should have a checkpoint for each stage of the policy process

The checkpoints are as follows:

For effective policy planning,
- Have you identified the true nature(issue) of the problem?
- Would the problem require government intervention; Is it inevitable?
- Have you check and thoroughly investigate the previous or similar policy cases?
- Have you identified and listened carefully to the related target population or groups?

For effective policy making,
- Did you make choice with your best option?
- Have you checked the resources necessary for the policy: Is it enough?

- Have you checked the related agencies and take prior consultation with them?
- Have you checked and followed the legal procedures?
- Have you set up the PR Plan?

For an effective policy announcement,
- Did you take consultation and coordination with your related parties?

For an effective policy implementation,
- Did you consistently maintain the policy priority?
- Have you strategically positioned the authorities and resources required for policy implementation?
- Have you monitored the responses of the policy target group from time to time and respond aptly?
- Did you perform monitoring at the mid-point of the policy implementation such that policy implements according to the original purpose?

For an effective policy evaluation,
- Do you realize your original policy goal?
- Do you set up the rewards and incentives(positive as well as negative) based upon policy evaluation?
- Do you make a document as a nice lively policy case and try to get some policy implications and policy learning.

| Figure 1-11 | EFFECTIVE POLICY MAKING: CHECK POINTS |

Rational Model	Check List	Cf
Policy Planning	• Have you identified the true nature(issue) finding of the problem? • Would the problem require government intervention; Is it inevitable? • Have you check and thoroughly investigate the previoussimilar policy cases? • Have you identified and listen carefully from the related target population or groups?	
Policy Making	• Did you make choice with your best option? • Have you checked the resources necessary for the policy: Is it enough? • Have you checked the related agencies and take a prior consultations with them? • Have you checked and followed the legal procedures? • Have you set up the PR plan?	
Policy Announcement	• Did you take consultation and coordination with your related parties?	
Policy Implementation	• Did you maintain the policy priority in a consistent manner? • Have you strategically positioned the authorities and resources required for policy implementation? • Have you monitored the responses of policy target group from time to time and respond aptly? • Did you perform monitoring at the mid-point of the policy implementation such that policy implements accordance to the original purport?	
Policy Evaluation	• Do you realize your original policy goal? • Do you set up the rewards and incentives(positive as well as negative) based upon policy evaluation? • Do you make a document as a nice lively policy case and try to get some policy implication and policy learning.	

9. Effective Policy Making: Korean Governance Case

The following figure shows the Korean case of policy life cycle governance. It is characterized by its successful identification for client needs, performance indicators, and policy validity. Also, it is the best case for a careful and meticulous policy quality control, and process innovation. For an effective agenda-setting and conceptualization of policy, the Korean government successfully performs a lot of tool-kits that include brainstorming, policy survey, SWOT, client needs, goal setting, process map, CSF, and resource plan. For effective policy making, the Korean government successfully performs concretization by utilizing feasibility study, scenario planning, PR planning, and opinion gathering as real-time management. For an effective policy confirmation, the Korean President resides a regular cabinet meeting at the Blue House(President Office) and closely consults with Parliament about strategic direction and policy making to enhance a successful policy performance. For an effective policy implementation and evaluation, the Korean government performs monitoring in the middle of implementation or by evaluating post-mortem performance.

| Figure 1-12 | KOREA: EFFECTIVE POLICY MAKING MODEL |

GOV POLICY LIFE CYCLE GOVERNANCE

* Client Needs, Performance Indicator, Policy Validity
* Best Practice, Policy Quality Control, Process Innovation

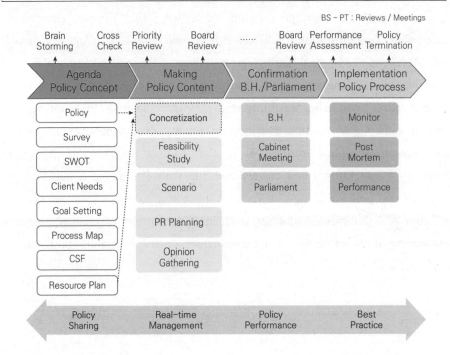

10. COVID-19, Korean Case for an Effective Policy Framework

As the coronavirus spreads rapidly around the world, killing thousands and leaving governments scrambling to deal with the fallout, one country has repeatedly drawn praise for its efficiency in dealing with it. **South Korea**.

Medical system or effective leadership, learning from past experiences?

South Korea has been praised for its response to the novel coronavirus disease (COVID-19), which combines widespread testing with innovative strategies such as public "drive-through" that separate a medical professional and patient and can provide results within several hours. Additionally, there have been efforts in triangulating available public and private data to track patients' whereabouts and schedules. The United States, recognizing South Korea's success, has even requested equipment, likely including test kits, from South Korea. The Moon Jae-in administration built upon South Korea's previous experiences responding to outbreaks of both Severe Acute Respiratory Syndrome(SARS) in 2003 and Middle East Respiratory Syndrome(MERS) in 2015.

South Korea is one of the few countries that succeeded in flattening the coronavirus curve. The policies of testing, tracing, and treating without lockdowns have been widely lauded. Some attribute this to South Korea's experience of having dealt with previous epidemics such as SARS and MERS. Commentators in the US tend to stress the country's effective leadership, contrasting it with that of Donald Trump's. Others point to cultural factors, such as the willingness of the public to sacrifice privacy for the greater public good.

Effective Governance and Agile Policy System

What is often overlooked, though, is that at the fundamental foundations of South Korea's success against Covid-19 are effective and efficient governance and policy systems to deliver its public services. Without this firm foundation and strong infrastructures, which was initiated under the leadership of President Park Chung Hee, the policy of test, trace, and treat could not have been sustained or expanded to the degree that it has. Furthermore, effective leadership cannot achieve much if it lacks a well-functioned public service system that can deliver.

In retrospect, South Korea, as a newly industrialized and independent developing country after World War II, brought not only state-led economic development but also new kinds of government-led medical implementations. During the 1950s, many South Koreans were still unfamiliar with Western medicine and did not initially welcome official health programs.

This began to change under the strong leadership of Park Chung Hee who brought the economic miracle of Han River. The strong and committed South Korean leader launched public health campaigns that fundamentally changed both the medical profession and the public's attitude toward it. New professional standards were demanded of doctors and their support staff, while the public was encouraged to participate in the medical and health insurance system and other state-organized health implementations.

Effective Smart ICT Infrastructure and Transparent System

Today, the Moon Jae-in government's response to the virus has not been without flaws and criticism. The South Korean media has blamed him for not moving quickly enough to ban Chinese tourists when the virus began spreading rapidly. Others have criticized the high degree of state surveillance. The government would have had far more difficulty carrying out contact tracing if it could not have closely followed the movement of its citizens through their smartphones and well-functioned credit card systems. This last point has quite critical implications because it implies the effective smart ICT infrastructure and transparent big data tracing system, which was an excellent smart foundation of South Korea's success stories.

Comprehensive and Systematic Policy Capacity

In a nutshell, South Korea's response to the recently emerged COVID-19 crisis was a success of Korean governance system and in specific, a comprehensive and systematic policy capacity: 1) Consistent Tracing the patients' whereabouts and schedules, 2) Transparent data opening to the public, 3) Citizen's cooperative attitude to the Government policy guidelines, 4) A Comprehensive and systematic test-kits Program, 5) Most importantly, An effective governance system and an improved policy capacity learned from the past policy experiences of SARSs and MERS.

What This Korean Story Implies to the Other Developing Nations?

Then, what this Korean story tells to the other developing countries? Of course, each country has different historical trajectories so that there is no one best solution or panacea. The best solution for a country, oftentimes, does not fit to the other nation. Nevertheless, one thing is clear, a strong state with a responsible and responsive leadership is always the answer. We are living in the age of turbulence, surrounded by very volatile, uncertain, complex, and ambiguous circumstances. We are not very sure about what kinds of wicked viruses or other unknown hazards will attack our life. In this regard, we need, more than ever before, agile governance, fully armed with effective policy frameworks and digital capacities.

11. Comprehensive Design: Effective Policy Making

To elucidate the holistic paradigm of effective policy making, we need to understand the following comprehensive design. Public policy has two aspects – i.e., rational and political. To upgrade its rational scientific features, the government should enhance its capacity building, from policy making, policy analysis, foresight and forecasting, and innovation theory. To harmonize its political features, the government should enhance its capacity building, from conflict management, attitude change, and new governance theory. This means that the government needs to integrate harmoniously its efficiency and democratic dimensions. Furthermore, the government should understand the uppermost dimension of reflexivity by studying smart e-Government theory. In total, effective policy making is the underpinning of good governance achieving

| Figure 1-13 | Effective Policy Making(5) |

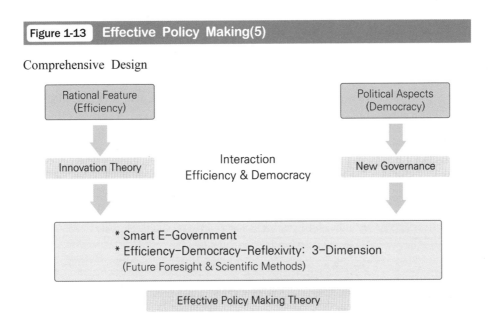

Comprehensive Design

efficiency, democracy, and reflexivity.

12. Summary and Conclusion: Effective Policy Making

Let's summarize the key lessons from this chapter.

The unfolding of the 21st century has brought the world into a new and different switch. As globalization and the 4th industrial revolution deepen in this contemporary age, uncertainty and complexity of wicked problems are ever heightened. It is the age of time, speed and uncertainty, or the turbulent age of volatility, uncertainty, complexity, and ambiguity. Under this age of turbulence, innovation is crucial to achieving the transformation of governance under society 4.0. To achieve innovation and transformation, effective policy making is indispensable. As we saw vividly in the vortex of COVID-19 crisis, smart governance based on effective policy making and implementation could save thousands of valuable human lives. As shown in the Korean successful cases, agile governance with effective policy making was the key to the answers. By utilizing big data and evidence-based scientific analyses which can lead to effective policy making, we can open a bright and more creative future to make a strong and great nation.

Figure 1-14 Summary & Conclusion: Effective Policy Making

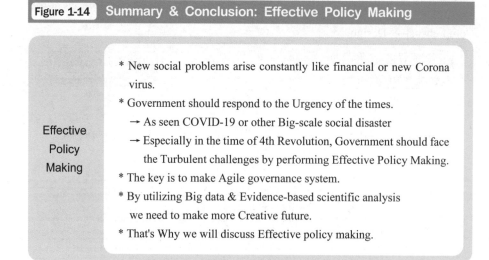

Effective Policy Making

* New social problems arise constantly like financial or new Corona virus.
* Government should respond to the Urgency of the times.
   → As seen COVID-19 or other Big-scale social disaster
   → Especially in the time of 4th Revolution, Government should face the Turbulent challenges by performing Effective Policy Making.
* The key is to make Agile governance system.
* By utilizing Big data & Evidence-based scientific analysis we need to make more Creative future.
* That's Why we will discuss Effective policy making.

Key Point!

1. Effective Policy Making and New Governance

▶ For the most developing nation, the dream of national innovation is to achieve a great and strong nation.

▶ This dream and vision start with effective policy making as the great nation should be built upon effective policy making and a strong foundation of the governance system.

2. Effective Policy Making and Capacity Building

▶ To become a strong and great nation, the governments, especially in the developing countries, need a new capacity building to enhance the government officials' capacity for effective policy making.

▶ For this purpose, some key agenda of the capacity building should be:
  • Identify "fundamental problems" faced in your society.
  • Perform evidence-based policy analysis and policy making
  • Learn the foundation of policy science with Smart e-Government, e-Transformation, and Attitude change for the behavioral perspectives.

3. Strong and Great Nation: Dimension

▶ There are five capitals that a nation needs to build up in this creative knowledge society. They are economic and physical capital, human capital, social capital, positive psychology capital, and spiritual capital.

4. Strong and Great Nation: Policy Criteria

▶ The policy criteria for good governance are composed of efficiency, democracy, and reflexivity.

▶ *Efficiency*. The strong and great nation should be strong and efficient. It should perform effective policy making.

▶ *Democracy*. The strong and great nation is a democratic nation. From the political and process standpoint, democracy is valuable and indispensable. It indicates not only political participation through election or voting but also participation in the policy making employing features of digital government.

▶ *Reflexivity*. The strong and great nation is reflexive. Reflexivity is a philosophical term. It refers to a supreme vision that a nation-state could realize. It is the highest dimension of effective policy making.

5. Effective Policy Making: Check Points for Quality Control

▶ For an effective policy making government need to have a tool-kit for policy quality management. To ensure policy success, effective policy making should have a checkpoint for each stage of the policy process.

▶ The checkpoints are as follows:

EFFECTIVE POLICY MAKING: CHECK POINTS

Rational Model	Check List	Cf
Policy Planning	• Have you identified the true nature(issue) finding of the problem? • Would the problem require government intervention; Is it inevitable? • Have you check and thoroughly investigate the previoussimilar policy cases? • Have you identified and listen carefully from the related target population or groups?	
Policy Making	• Did you make choice with your best option? • Have you checked the resources necessary for the policy: Is it enough? • Have you checked the related agencies and take a prior consultations with them? • Have you checked and followed the legal procedures? • Have you set up the PR plan?	
Policy Announcement	• Did you take consultation and coordination with your related parties?	

Policy Implementation	• Did you maintain the policy priority in a consistent manner? • Have you strategically positioned the authorities and resources required for policy implementation? • Have you monitored the responses of policy target group from time to time and respond aptly? • Did you perform monitoring at the mid-point of the policy implementation such that policy implements accordance to the original purport?
Policy Evaluation	• Do you realize your original policy goal? • Do you set up the rewards and incentives(positive as well as negative) based upon policy evaluation? • Do you make a document as a nice lively policy case and try to get some policy implication and policy learning.

6. Effective Policy Making: Korean Governance Case

▶ For an effective agenda-setting and policy concept, the Korean government successfully performs a lot of tool-kits that include brainstorming, policy survey, SWOT, client needs, goal setting, process map, CSF, and resource plan.

▶ For effective policy making, the Korean government successfully performs concretization by utilizing feasibility study, scenario planning, PR planning, and Opinion gathering as real-time management.

▶ For an effective policy confirmation, the Korean President resides a regular cabinet meeting at the Blue House(President Office) and closely consults with Parliament about strategic direction and policy making to enhance a successful policy performance.

▶ For an effective policy implementation and evaluation, the Korean government performs monitoring in the middle of implementation or by evaluating post-mortem performance.

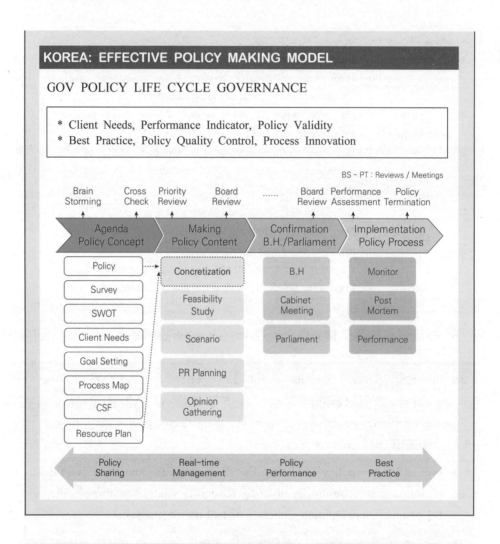

KOREA: EFFECTIVE POLICY MAKING MODEL

GOV POLICY LIFE CYCLE GOVERNANCE

* Client Needs, Performance Indicator, Policy Validity
* Best Practice, Policy Quality Control, Process Innovation

BS ~ PT : Reviews / Meetings

| Brain Storming | Cross Check | Priority Review | Board Review | ...... | Board Review | Performance Assessment | Policy Termination |

| Agenda Policy Concept | Making Policy Content | Confirmation B.H./Parliament | Implementation Policy Process |

Policy	Concretization	B.H	Monitor
Survey	Feasibility Study	Cabinet Meeting	Post Mortem
SWOT			
Client Needs	Scenario	Parliament	Performance
Goal Setting	PR Planning		
Process Map			
CSF	Opinion Gathering		
Resource Plan			

| Policy Sharing | Real-time Management | Policy Performance | Best Practice |

Figure 1-15   **Discussion Question: Effective Policy Making**

| Effective Policy Making | • What is effective policy making?
 • Why we need it?
 • What if you cannot meet it? What if not effective?
 • What is the Policy Science Framework to address these issues? |

Chapter 2

ATTITUDE CHANGE
The Behavioral Approach for Effective Policy Making

Attitude change will make your mindset, and guide you to the great success with big fortune. Attitude is more important than the reality. More important than your appearance, capacity and talents. It is the mission critical to your success in the fields of your business, family, friendship, and organization.

Suh Yoon Lee, Author, Global bestseller, <The Having>

✎ ››› Objectives

The purpose of this chapter is to elucidate the paradigm of attitude change.

This chapter focuses on the theoretical foundation of attitude change and its relationship with effective policy making. It will be especially helpful for government officials in the developing countries because it will contribute not only to their policy scheme but more importantly to the personal success and happiness in their life.

First, it will highlight the relationship between attitude change and effective policy making.

Second, it will put emphasis on the holistic understanding of attitude change using brain science, old oriental wisdom, and modern positive psychology.

Third, it will reexamine the successful conditions for effective policy making with a focus on analyzing the Korean economic policy success.

Finally, it will elucidate the negative attitudes prevailing in the developing countries and present some strategic solutions to overcome those negative attitudes to accomplish more effective policy making.

Attitude Change and Effective Policy Making

The framework of effective policy making needs three components: technology, process, and attitude change. Among them, attitude change is the core. Without attitude change and mindset, national innovation in the developing area will be futile. Just like a human being is composed of physical body, mind, and soul, national development requires technological innovation, process management, and creative attitude change.

Effective policy making could present
1) efficiency
2) accountability
3) agility and speedy solution, and
4) responsiveness to the target group in the society

To achieve this vision, we need a strong foundation of technological infrastructure, good management of policy process (with the aid of financial and human resources) and the most importantly, dedicated attitude of people with special guidance of strong and committed leadership.

Heeks (2004, 2013) found that the success rate of e-government in developing countries is only 15%, while the failure rate is as much as 85%. Among the failure, 35% of them are total failure and 50% are partial failure. He identified many reasons for failure in implementing e-government, starting with the lack of education and awareness, weakness in cooperation within the organization to lead efforts, and to clarify the organization's new direction, the ambiguity of vision, and poor communication channels. Moran(2013; 1998:39) aptly put it this way: the plans in the developing countries fall into one of the two categories: vision without substance and a budget without vision.

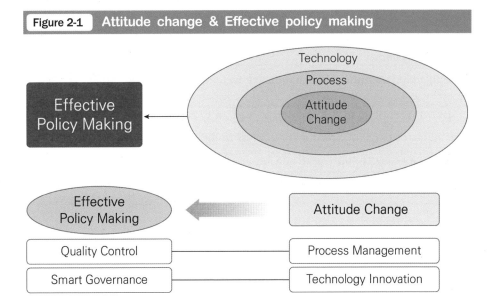

Figure 2-1 Attitude change & Effective policy making

Effective

Policy Making: ① Efficiency ② Accountability ③ Agility ④ Responsiveness

What is Attitude Change? Mindfulness and Conviction

What is an attitude change, then?

Human being shows three distinctive behaviors: think, talk, and act.. In a broader sense, attitude or mindset encompasses the way we talk, the way we perceive or think, and the way we act (style and habit of doing things). One may easily determine the mindset (either negative or positive), cheerful or depressive, grateful or complaining by observing an individual's way of talking, thinking, and overall behavior towards a particular stimuli. So, the way you eat, exercise, study, pray, and work shows your attitude.

Belief System

If this kind of attitude is accumulated, we call it a belief system.

Belief, according to the dictionary, is literally defined as "an attitude toward a certain fact or person." Spiritually, it refers to the situation that a person conforms his life or attitudes to the Supreme God or some Transcendent Being. Our internal landscape is continuously being changed by this kind of belief and will affect our actions and behaviors. In short, our life and destiny are folding out, according to the blueprint that we actually believe.

The belief that a person holds is shaped by experiences gained from earlier life – i.e., interaction with family, education, and social environment. Some belief is so positive and powerful enough to propel one's personal life toward a successful career; or even further to identify his true self. Some belief, on the other hand, is working so negatively to devastate life.

Let's ponder about for a moment: What about my belief system? Is it working positively or negatively?

Stay calm and silent. Squarely look at your inner-mind and carefully reflect on it. The belief makes you who you are; and such belief will change your future as it will transform your innermost mindset and attitudes.

Strong Conviction

A deeper and strong belief, we call it conviction. Once engraved within your sub-consciousness mind, the conviction will change and transform your life. And it will make you identify your true self.

This is obviously the most critical factor in your life. It is quite different from just a material success which satisfies only your physical desires.

Stay calm and still. And notice a clear awareness of within your consciousness. The external world is a reflection of your belief and conviction. If your mindset has been changed, your outcome will be changed accordingly. Because the changed attitude and mindset will transform you so that you will become a different person and react differently to the external signals even though the environment remains the same. A successful person keeps a "Having Mind", which is basically "gratitude, joyful and grateful mind," to always feel an abundant and grateful mind in the face of whatever hardship and ordeals in life.

The Secret Behind Success

If you possess a strong conviction, you will achieve great success. Strong belief gives you great confidence, then again leading to a strong conviction. Confidence refers to a subjective condition but conviction is based on facts and truths.

The secret behind success is as follows: First, you have to understand that you are not just a physical body, instead you are a spiritual being. Your Spirit contains your mental mind that is basically acting as the blueprint guiding your life; your *mind* (software) is the control tower of your *body* (hardware). An individual who has a stronger conviction will definitely achieve greater success because he possesses the stronger blue chips in his mind.

You should remember that your *mind is* the master of your body. In other words, your mind is the master of your brain, cardiac, and the other organs, even the whole cells. Therefore, the person with a greater conviction will always be the winner. The strong conviction commands your brain and will achieve your goal without any resistance by attracting, like a powerful magnet, all the possible means, and opportunities around you.

Mindfulness & Conviction

So here is an assignment for you, a practical exercise in transforming your life: Do the Mindfulness and Conviction Exercise. It will change your life.

- **Stay Calm, Still, and Silence**
- **Notice There is a Clear Awareness within Your Consciousness**
- **A Deeper and Strong Conviction will Transform Yourself.**
- **It will also enable you to Identify your True Self.**

Figure 2-2 Attitude Change: Mindfulness & Conviction

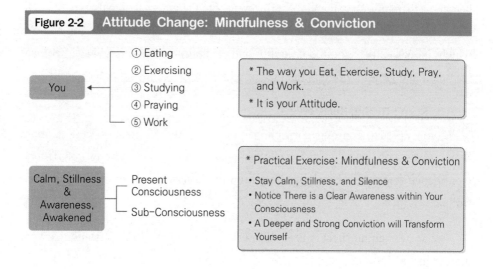

⏹ Attitude Change: Conviction and Consciousness

The *conviction* is fundamentally decided by your *consciousness*. Your consciousness has two components – i.e., *present consciousness and sub consciousness* – that contains two levels of vibration: high or low. When you have low vibrations, your present consciousness shows much small noisy thinking, ego-based anxiety, or complaints, keep asking attention to your body and mind. Also, when you have low vibrations, your sub consciousness is boring, dull, and tedious with some fear and anxiety. In this situation, naturally, you cannot have a strong conviction.

The solution to these low-vibrational statuses is to upgrade your consciousness level: Block+Deep:
1) **Block** out any external noisy and stressful minds; and
2) Make a **Deep** change by entering into your deep consciousness level

Change the channels of your present consciousness, from noisy and asking small ego minds to calm and stillness, and empty and silence, which is basically peaceful and tranquil. At the same time, change channels of your sub consciousness from boring, dull, and sleepy to a clear, awareness, and awakened mind. We call this practice as mindfulness exercise.

In conclusion, your uppermost high-level consciousness is Pure-consciousness, having two characteristics: One dimension is calm, stillness, empty, and silence for the present consciousness; and the other dimension is clear, attention, awareness, and awakened mind for the sub consciousness. In short, your pure consciousness is calm and awakened, and empty but full of awareness. This is very important and I hope you will remember and practice the mindfulness exercise!

Figure 2-3	Attitude Change: Conviction & Consciousness

① Noisy, Asking ➡ Clam, Stillness

② Boring, Sleepy ➡ Awareness, Awakened ➡ Mindfulness
(Super-Consciousness)

- Practical Exercise: Mindfulness & Conviction
  ▶ Find out the Pure-Consciousness, Where is it in your Mind?
  ▶ Find out who you really are: Calm, Stillness + Awareness, Awakened
    = Mindfulness(Super-Consciousness)
- Stay Calm, Stillness, and Silence
- Notice There is a Clear Awareness within Your Consciousness
- A Deeper and Strong Conviction will Transform Yourself

Attitude Change: Do your Best Even the Small Things

In oriental tradition, the old wisdom dictates, "Do your best even if it is the small things." These kinds of small attitude and mindset will eventually lead to your great success in your career.

The following paragraph is quoted by <Jung Yong>, the famous ancient classic book, widely read by the intelligent ruling class in the old dynasty of Korea. It highlights the essence of truth, saying that the small attitude change will harvest greater returns.

It says:

Figure 2-4   Attitude change: Do your best even the small things

Do Your Best even though it is a small thing.
If you do the best, your mind will become sincere.

Mind attitude sincere, it will become expressed.
If expressed, it will be manifested.

If manifested, it will become brighter.
If brighter and enlightened, it will touch other people.

If you touched other people, it will be changed
If it changed, it will grow

Therefore, the one who do one's best in his own work,
Will transform himself and change the world.

* Jung Yong, The Ancient Korean Bible, the 23th Section

Attitude Change: How Creativity Getting Started?

Modern brain science tells that the human brain has three-components,
    (1) the new cortex for reason and rationality
    (2) midbrain of the limbic system for emotion and feeling, and
    (3) brain stem for the most fundamental life essence and vital energy

It is important to notice that there is a small system in the brain stem called Reticular Activating System (RAS). It is basically a filtering system and it is valuable to know that once your will and commitment successfully engraved in this filter system, you will be determined to attain your vision and goal whatever it will be. That's why at least 21 days for determination or praying is so much important to change your small attitude and mindset, which will eventually change your destiny and life.

So, now let's check our attitude and mind. There are four crucial evaluative questions to check focusing on joyfulness, positivity, creativity, and being deep:

1) Are you joyful?

2) Do you have a positive outlook

3) Are you creative? and

4) Are you deeply focused?

These four critical questions will find you whether you are a really happy person or not; and whether you are a really creative person or not.

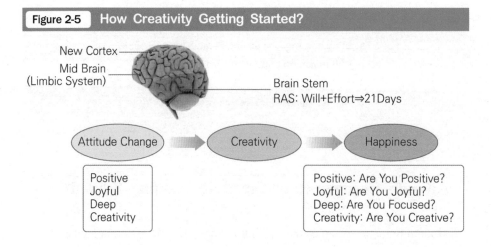

Figure 2-5 | **How Creativity Getting Started?**

Creative Insight: Block+Deep

The formula for creative insight is Block+Deep. It means that Block other noises and go to deep thinking.

It is so critical in attaining the level of deep change. If you want to realize deep change, change your present mind to stillness and silence. And change your potential mind to a more clear, succinct, and awakened.

It will ensure your creative insight and creativity, which will definitely lead to effective policy making and maybe more importantly leading to your great personal success as it will provide the strong mental foundation for greater wealth and fortune in your life.

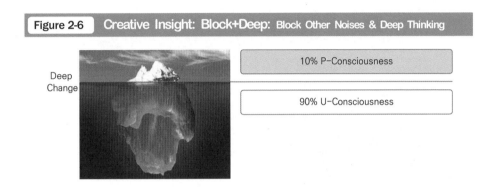

Figure 2-6 | Creative Insight: Block+Deep: Block Other Noises & Deep Thinking

Deep Change

10% P-Consciousness

90% U-Consciousness

Critical Tip(1): Raise a Question-type Affirmation

If your unconsciousness conflicts with your belief, then *affirmation* do not work. For example, if you are doing the *affirmation* such as "I am a rich person, I am very attractive" then suddenly you might have a skeptical feeling sprouting from your deep unconsciousness that, "Am I"? It means that your innermost mind, called unconsciousness mind, shows a strong resistance. We call it self-criticism.

But what if you raise an *affirmation* type of question? It will diminish that resistance. Further, our brain system always has a tendency that provides the answers when a question is being raised. Therefore, the *affirmation* type of question, utilizing these kinds of characteristics, never fails to find your answer and execute it to the end without much resistance. That's how our brain system works. Hence, let's perform and constantly keep, or as much as you can, raising an affirmation question-type. This is another practical exercise for you to realize your vision and dream. The samples are as follows:

- **Why I am so successful?**
- **Why I am so effective and strong?**
- **Why I am getting rich?**
- **Why I am so attractive?**

Figure 2-7 Creative Tip(1): Raise a Question-type Affirmation for a Deep Thinking

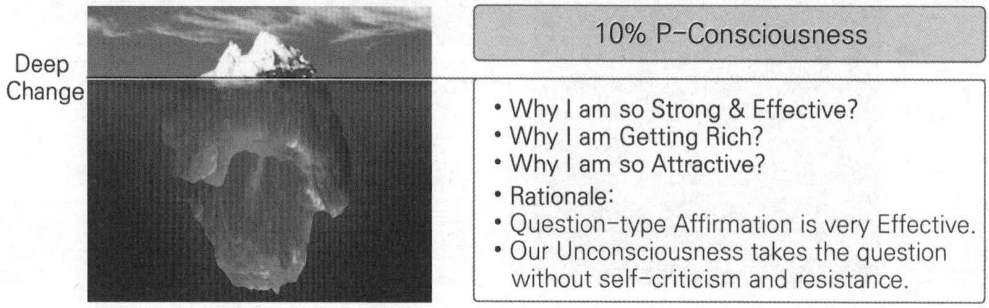

Critical Tip(2): Find the Common Characteristics of a Great Fortune

There exists a clear common characteristic among the persons who possess a great fortune whether it is through money, getting a promotion, or great achievement. Great wealth and happiness are obviously flowing from those achievements. Find and notice those common characteristics so that you could benchmark:

- **Focusing on the Positive Aspects**
- **Having Gratitude Feelings**
- **Great Confidence**
- **Joyful Attitudes**
- **Pouring the Best Efforts before God's Decision and Judgment**

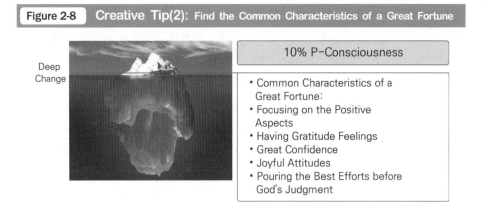

Figure 2-8 Creative Tip(2): Find the Common Characteristics of a Great Fortune

Deep Change

10% P-Consciousness

- Common Characteristics of a Great Fortune:
- Focusing on the Positive Aspects
- Having Gratitude Feelings
- Great Confidence
- Joyful Attitudes
- Pouring the Best Efforts before God's Judgment

Critical Tip(3): Find Your Pure Consciousness: The Essence of Life Force

At one point, you were the essence of the life force itself. Think about a newly-born baby, the life force within the new baby was shining, crystalizing, and loving existence. It existed within the physical external appearance. It is vibrating frequencies, a high level of consciousness, and is life energy in itself. As time goes on, and as you are getting age, you had to face many external circumstances: you have to survive in this world so that it is inevitable to compete with each other fiercely sometimes. The life force, once very flexible, empty but vast, pure with loving characteristics, became rigid, full of egos, contaminated with a lot of selfishness. Your self-image and ego became fixed. Sometimes, you may have a feeling that your shining life energy has gone or fading, or even sometimes forget completely whether that kind of thing existed.

But the truth is, it is not; your life essence is still shining vividly within your Mind and Consciousness. The only problem is that you just forgot the existence in the vortex of life or death survival game in this neo-liberal society. The good news is, it is not the thing evading or falling out.

But you have to put our best efforts to find and keep it in your daily life. You need to find the shining life force within your Mind. It is high time to be wake up and awakened because you have your Pure Consciousness or True Self within your Mind and Consciousness: Shining and Awakened, Stillness with Awareness, and Empty but full of Wisdom and Loving force.

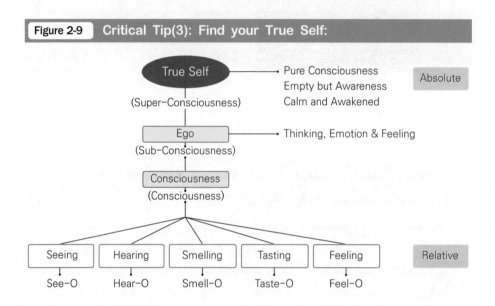

Figure 2-9 Critical Tip(3): Find your True Self:

Critical Tip(4): Pure Consciousness will Create Your Reality

Pure Consciousness will create your reality by using your body and mind. So let's ponder about the relationship between Consciousness and individual body and mind.

The diagram below tells you the fundamental truth. Consciousness is eternal life; having infinite and abundant life energy. This energy is permeated in your body and mind, thus allowing you to create and experience your reality. During your stay in this world, the world is functioning like the Server of the Computer system. Your body and mind are logged in this Server 1 like a game character or avatar. When your story is over in this world, your body will passed away but not the soul. The Consciousness will allow you to plug in another Server, say Server 2. Because Consciousness has many other Servers like a multi-dimensional system in the Universe.

Hence, it is a Universal Life Energy and your Pure Consciousness is eternal, not the one to be passed away or fading out. The characteristics of this Pure Consciousness are 1) Calm, silence, stillness; and 2) vastly empty but always noticing with attention, therefore clear, awareness, and awakened.

The good news is that you can share and possess this pure energy in your soul. If you are really awakened, thus having a great conviction that you are a truly great being who possessed this spontaneous and fundamental life force, you will surely create and experience this greatness in your real life. So, bless your soul, healing, and give inspirations. And always select the thinking and ideas to give you vitality, happiness, and wellness with a full of joyful energy.

Figure 2-10 Creative Tip(4): Pure Consciousness will Create Your Reality

CONSCIOUSNESS(Infinite & Abundant Life Energy)
→ Body, Mind →erver1, Server2, ⋯, Server n
→ Create & Experience
    (Physical world, Non-physical world)

The Characteristics of PURE CONSCIOUSNESS:
1) Calm, Silence, Stillness
2) Clear, Awareness, Awakened

Critical Tip(5): Tentative Conclusion: Affirmation will Change Your Life

Now let's conclude tentatively and derive some conclusion for the sake of clarity.

We have noticed that our True Mind has two dimensions: one is calm and empty dimension, the other is awareness& awakened dimension. We called it True Self or Pure Consciousness.

When we perform Block+Deep, Block is to keep a calm and empty mind, and Deep is to have awareness and awakened mind.

Also, when we perform Affirmation, for example, "I am Strong and Powerful," this affirmation is the content of a positive and awakened mind. Therefore, it has the strong effect of proclaiming that "I am calm and empty basically but with full of strong & powerful mind."

This magic is very powerful and authentic and you will become such a strong and powerful personality one by one.

Therefore, let's do the Affirmation such as: Why I am so Healthy & Powerful? Or, Why I am so Lucky & Happy? It will upgrade your Consciousness level and will make you create a Healthy, Effective, Strong, and Powerful life.

Figure 2-11 Creative Tip(5): Tentative Conclusion: Affirmation will Change Your Life

Deep Change

10% P-Consciousness

- Why I am so Healthy & Powerful?
- Why I am so Lucky & Happy?
- Rationale:
- Affirmation will upgrade your Consciousness level.
- And will Make you to Create a Healthy, Effective, Strong & Powerful Life.

The Path of Your Successful Life: Who will be the Winner?

Who will be the winner in the game of life? Life is full of risky situations and a lot of difficult challenges--sometimes with a peaceful wind of sailing, but oftentimes we are facing a turbulent storm or hurricane. Then, maybe it is very meaningful to deduce the formula for a successful life if any.

Figure 2-12   The Path to Successful Life: Who will be the Winner?

The following diagram shows the equation for a successful career. It highlights a clear goal and vision with a strong desire. As I have mentioned already, the RAS has an important role here. If you have a clear vision with a consistent desire, it will be engraved in the RAS, then the goal will be surely attained. If you put a serious effort with a great passion, the achievement will give you self-trust and great confidence, which will lead to self-realization in your career. Then, you will be the winner in your life. Also, the government officials with this mind of great attitude will provide effective policy making which will surely lead to the great vision of national innovation.

Dynamic Cycle of Transformation: How to Achieve Excellence?

It is also very useful to note that excellence is the outcome of dynamic processes(Quinn, 1996).The state of excellence is a function of strong desire, vision, confidence, and practices. As the below diagram shows, to accomplish and maintain excellence, it is necessary to initiate a fundamental or deep change that associates with continuous experiments, risk-taking, and learning. To keep controlling negative side effects such as fear of failure, illusion, terror, slump, or exhaustion, an entrepreneur should attempt a repeated experiment and endeavors.

Particularly, the dynamic cycle of transformation includes the following steps: strong desire, vision, experiment, insight, confidence, synergy, mastery, and excellence. It also takes the following stages: initiation stage, uncertainty stage, transformation stage, and routine stage.

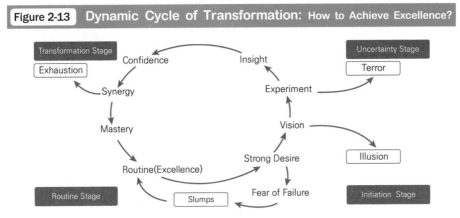

Figure 2-13 Dynamic Cycle of Transformation: How to Achieve Excellence?

* Revised from Robert E. Quinn, 〈Deep Change: Discovering the Leader Within〉, John Wiley & Sons, Inc.

From the initiation and experiments with a strong desire and vision, one can earn an insight and confidence, which will give him a greater synergy and mastery. As a result, one can achieve a state of proficiency and excellence as a routine stage. We call him a real master and will attain success, fortune, and real happiness.

The Core of Inner Mind: Calm and Awakened

It is very useful, at this moment, to recapitalize the inner structure of our mind. According to the famous psychologist, Ken Wilber(2016), our mind structure includes the following components: core, thinking, emotion, feeling, will and commitment. As shown in the figure below, the core of our inner mind is the most important for our behavior. It is so critical to have a clam and awakened mind in your innermost consciousness. If your mind is awakened at the core level, thinking, emotion, and feeling, the energy will be directed in the most appropriate way. Consequently, you have great energy with a high level of will and commitment. That's the basic framework for the attitude change.

Figure 2-14 The Core of Inner Mind: Calm & Awakened

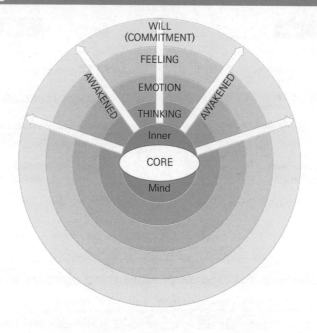

Level of Will(Commitment)

Level of Feeling(Feeling Energy)

Level of Emotion(Emotion Energy)

Level of Thinking(Thinking Energy)

CORE=INNER MIND

Institutional Approach to Overcome Negative Attitudes: Theoretical Modelling

As mentioned earlier, according to Heeks(2004, 2013), the success rate of e-government in the developing countries is only 15%, while the failure rate is as much as 85%. One of the key obstacles is the negative or inactive attitude such as *silos, sectionalism, comfort zone, or resistance to change* in these countries. Therefore, in the following section, let's discuss the problem and will try to offer practical solutions to overcome the negative attitudes from an institutional perspective.

First of all, let's consider the model explaining the job commitment in the organization (see figure below). The diagram shows that the X-axis is the level of capacity, while the Y-axis is the level of job difficulty or challenge. The 1st Quadrant is the ideal. It shows a high job difficulty level but having possessed a high level of capacity to tackle the problem. In this case, organizational members show high enthusiasm with a high return, showing a high job commitment. The 3rd Quadrant is the worst case. It shows a low job difficulty level and a low capacity. In this case, organizational members show no enthusiasm with minimal development, showing a depressive attitude. The 2nd Quadrant is an interesting case. It shows a high capacity but a low job difficulty level. In this case, organizational members show no enthusiasm because the work level is not challenging enough and they do not have much motivation, thus showing a boring or tedious attitude. The 4th Quadrant is the opposite case. It shows a high challenging level but with a low capacity. In this case, organizational members are burdened and stressed as the job level is too difficult for them. They may show high enthusiasm but gains low returns. Therefore, in this case, we can conclude as the situation of a passion without much development, which is also not desirable for the organization. This all implies that it is very important to assign the appropriate job to the organizational members by analyzing job classification in Personnel Management.

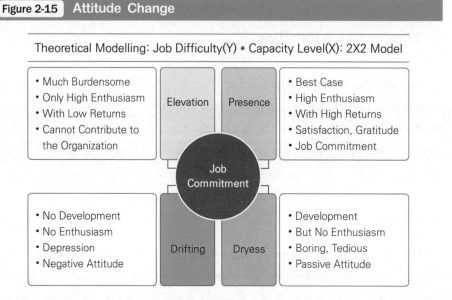

Figure 2-15 | Attitude Change

Theoretical Modelling: Job Difficulty(Y) * Capacity Level(X): 2X2 Model

• Much Burdensome • Only High Enthusiasm • With Low Returns • Cannot Contribute to the Organization	Elevation / Presence	• Best Case • High Enthusiasm • With High Returns • Satisfaction, Gratitude • Job Commitment
• No Development • No Enthusiasm • Depression • Negative Attitude	Drifting / Dryess	• Development • But No Enthusiasm • Boring, Tedious • Passive Attitude

Job Commitment

Public Official Innovation

Following the theoretical model discussed above, it is important to achieve public official innovation. For this purpose, we need a two-level approach: One with individual and culture, the other with organizational and technical. While putting many endeavors to achieve the organizational and technological innovation, for the purpose of individual and culture innovation we need to promote Self Motivation with Capacity Building.

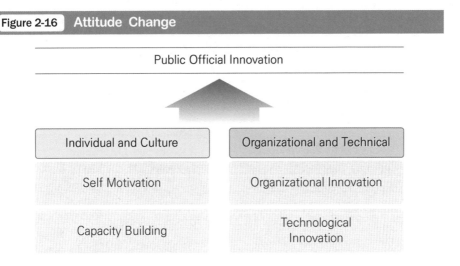

Figure 2-16 Attitude Change

Public Official Innovation

Individual and Culture

Self Motivation

Capacity Building

Organizational and Technical

Organizational Innovation

Technological Innovation

To improve Self Motivation, we need to have a training system approached by the position level. For example, for the working-level officials, the education program should be focused on the analytical methods such as cost-benefit and cost-effectiveness analysis as in this level problem definition and analytical approach is so critical. However, as the position moves up like the division director level, the education program should be focused on institutional building as in this level the agenda such as distributing incentives in a fair and effective way; how to promote an interactive communication with the line officers; or how to provide the relevant legal framework is so critical. As the position moves up to the director-general level, the education program should be focused on strategy setting as in this level the agenda such as leadership with a clear vision and direction is so critical.

Therefore, the capacity building will be differently approached: for the incoming officials and for the high-level officials or approached differently by the job grade and job classification. Also, fundamentally, it is very important to promote public value education by enhancing the dignity of public officials.

Figure 2-17	Attitude Change

Capacity Building Program

Self Motivation	Capacity Building
* Training System by Position Level 1) Problem Definition(Analysis, B/C, E/C, Regression) 2) Institutional Building(Incentives, Communication, Laws) 3) Strategy Setting(Leadership, Vision & Direction)	* Strengthening the Program for Incoming Officials • Strengthening the Training Program for Newly Employees * Strengthening the Capacity of High- level Officials • Strengthening the Training Program for High-level Officials * Spread of Public Value • Expanding Education on the Dignity of Public Officials

Organizational & Technical Innovation

In addition to the individual approach, it is also important to achieve organizational and technical innovation.

For the organizational innovation, we need two approaches:
1) Encouragement of Positive Administration
2) Innovation of the Work System.

For the encouragement of positive administration, we need to strengthen the discipline for the passive attitudes such as
1) Comfort Zone
2) Not Doing Anything
3) Passive Attitude, and
4) Bribery & Corruption

Also, it is important to take a Flexible Approach for the Good Mistake. For the innovation of the work system, we need to improve the work process by using BPR. Also, it is important to take a Balanced Approach of Work & Life.

For organizational innovation, we need two approaches:
1) Smart E-government
2) Improving Quality

For the Smart E-government, we need to maximize efficiency by using Smart E-government. Also for Improving Quality, we need to perform effective policy making while using big data and scientific policy analysis.

Figure 2-18 | **Attitude Change**

Organizational & Technical Innovation

Organizational Innovation	Technical Innovation

* Encouragement of Positive Administration
• Strengthening Discipline for Passive Attitude
    1) Comfort Zone
    2) Not Doing Anything
    3) Passive Attitude
    4) Bribery & Corruption
• Flexible Approach for the Good Mistake
 	
* Innovation of the Work System
• Improvement of Work Process using BPR
• Balanced Approach of Work & Life
	* Smart E-government
	• Maximizing Efficiency by Using Smart E-government
	
	* Improving Quality
	• By Performing Effective Policy Making
	• By Using Big Data & Scientific Policy Analysis

Summary and Conclusion: Attitude Change and Effective Policy Making

Let's summarize the key contents of this chapter.

In this chapter, we highlight the paradigm of attitude change and argue that attitude change is so much critical to attaining effective policy making, either at an individual level or government level.

As globalization and the 4th industrial revolution deepen in this contemporary age, the uncertainty from the wicked problems such as the COVID-19 crisis is ever heightened. As uncertainty is ever increasing, it is more important to have a clear and awakened mind to have better and effective policy making.

Generally, there are many negative attitudes. Among others, the most major negative attitudes in the developing countries are as follows:

   1) Red-Tape(Formalism)
   2) Misplacement of Goals and Means
   3) Easy-going Attitude
   4) Nepotism
   5) Sectionalism(Silos)
   6) Dependence Too Much on Boss Authority
   7) Trained Incapacity, and
   8) Resistance to Change

Figure 2-19 | Attitude Change

Negative Attitude

Main Negative factors
Red-Tape(Formalism) Misplacement of Goals and Means Easy-going Attitude Nepotism Sectionalism(Silos) Dependence Too Much on Boss Authority Trained Incapacity Resistance to Change

Effective
Policy Making

Inside & Outside

Inside Circumstance	Outside Circumstance
• Paradigm Change ▶ Passive Attitude, Risk Aversion ▶ Active Attitude, Risk Initiatives	• Knowledge–based Economy ▶ Globalization ▶ New Crisis, COVID–19

These are all important hurdles to effective policy making. To overcome these obstacles, at a personal level, we need to be armed with clear professionalism and positive psychology. At the cultural level, we need to perform attitude change:

(1) Old Thinking vs. New Initiatives

(2) Analogue vs. Digital

(3) Only Following Law vs. Entrepreneur Attempts, and

(4) Public Administration vs. New Management.

In other words, we need to change from old analog thinking to more digital entrepreneurship, from past-oriented minds to more future-oriented initiatives, and from public administration bureaucratic mind to a more new public management innovation.

For the organization level, we need to perform effective policy management including effective agenda-setting and policy making, and effective implementation &evaluation. Lastly, for the technical level, we need a strong ICT infrastructure and smart government foundation in which digital governance with knowledge creation and learning will be most beautifully flourished.

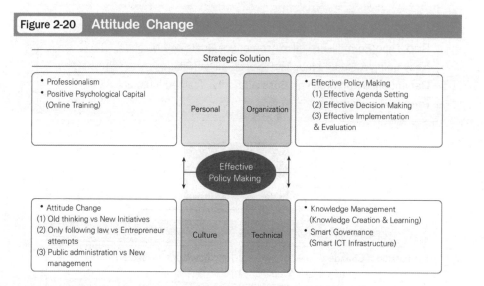

Figure 2-20 Attitude Change

Key Point!

1. Attitude Change and Effective Policy Making

▶ The framework of effective policy making needs three components: technology, process, and attitude change. Among them, attitude change is the core.

Strong Conviction

▶ A deeper and strong belief, we call it Conviction. Once engraved within your Sub-consciousness mind, the Conviction will change and transform your life. And it will make you identify your True Self.

The Secret Behind Success

▶ The strong conviction commands to his brain and will achieve his goal without any failure by attracting, like a powerful Magnet, all the possible means, and opportunities around him.

Mindfulness & Conviction

▶ So here is my practical exercise assignment for your life-changing: Do the Mindfulness & Conviction Exercise. It will change your life.

• Stay Calm, Stillness, and Silence

• Notice There is a Clear Awareness within Your Consciousness

• A Deeper and Strong Conviction will Transform Yourself.

• It will also Make you to Identify your True Self.

2. Creative Insight: Block+Deep

▶ The formula for creative insight is Block+Deep. It means that Block other noises and goes to deep thinking.

▶ It will ensure your creative insight and creativity, which will definitely lead to effective policy making and maybe, more importantly, leading to your great personal success.

Critical Tip(1): Raise a Question-type Affirmation

▶ The question-type Affirmation never fails to find your answer and execute it to the end without much resistance. The samples are as follows:
- Why I am so successful?
- Why I am so effective and strong?
- Why I am getting rich?
- Why I am so attractive?

Critical Tip(2): Find the Common Characteristics of a Great Fortune

▶ There exist clear common characteristics among the persons who possess a great fortune. Find and notice those common characteristics so that you could benchmark:
- Focusing on the Positive Aspects
- Having Gratitude Feelings
- Great Confidence
- Joyful Attitudes
- Pouring the Best Efforts before God's Decision & Judgment

Critical Tip(3): Find Your Pure Consciousness: The Essence of Life Force

▶ You need to find the shining life force within your Mind. It is high time to be wake up and awakened. Because you have your Pure Consciousness or True Self within your Mind and Consciousness: Shining and Awakened, Stillness with Awareness, and Empty but full of Wisdom and Loving force.

Critical Tip(4): Tentative Conclusion: Affirmation will Change Your Life

▶ This magic is very powerful and authentic. And you will become such a strong and powerful personality one by one.

▶ Therefore, let's do the Affirmation such as: Why I am so Healthy & Powerful? Or, Why I am so Lucky & Happy?

▶ It will upgrade your Consciousness level and will make you create a Healthy, Effective, Strong, and Powerful life.

3. Attitude Change and Effective Policy Making

▶ There are many negative attitudes. Among others, the most major negative attitudes in the developing countries are as follows: 1) Red-Tape(Formalism), 2) Misplacement of Goals and Means, 3) Easy-going Attitude, 4) Nepotism, 5) Sectionalism(Silos), 6) Dependence Too Much on Boss Authority,7) Trained Incapacity, and 8) Resistance to Change.

▶ To overcome these obstacles, at a personal level, we need to be armed with clear professionalism and positive psychology.

▶ At the cultural level, we need to perform attitude change: (1) Old Thinking vs New Initiatives, (2) Analogue vs Digital, (3) Only Following Law vs Entrepreneur Attempts, and (4) Public Administration vs New Management.

Practical Exercise: Attitude Change

Attitude Change

- Practical Exercise: Mindfulness & Conviction
- ➢ Find out the Pure-Consciousness. Where is it in your Mind?
- ➢ Find out who you really are. What is your True Self and Where is it in your Mind? What are those two dimensions?
  Calm, Stillness + Awareness, Awakened = Mindfulness(Super-Consciousness)

  * Stay Calm, Stillness, and Silence.
  * Notice There is a Clear Awareness within Your Mind.
  * A Deeper and Strong Conviction will Transform Yourself.

- ➢ Discuss how you can change your Mind to a Calm, Silence & Awakened. What kind of practice would be the Best Exercise?

Chapter 3

SMART POLICY FRAMEWORK 4.0

The Structural Approach for Effective Policy Making

Smart Policy Framework 4.0 is the most updated paradigm for effective policy making. Therefore it is so critical framework for the national innovation of the developing countries.

📝 ››› **Objectives**

The purpose of this chapter is to explain the smart policy framework 4.0. It is to provide a new structural perspective of effective policy making by comparing the traditional way and the modern way, or by comparison of governance 1.0, 2.0, 3.0, and 4.0.

First, it will highlight the relationship between smart policy framework and effective policy making.

Second, it will provide a holistic understanding of smart governance 4.0 by reviewing the previous governance model from 1.0 to 3.0.

Third, it will revisit the successful conditions for business process reengineering to provide a process-wise tool kit for effective policy making.

Finally, it will present the new model of smart policy framework 4.0 by addressing its vision and challenges.

The Structural Approach to Effective Policy Making: Traditional and Contemporary Approaches

To demonstrate the paradigm of effective policy making, we need to understand the administrative, policy, and governance model looking at both the traditional and contemporary approaches and delving on Governance transformation from the so-called Governance 1.0, 2.0, 3.0, and 4.0.

The traditional way is based on the old administrative system, which is basically a bureaucratic model. The basic operating mode is command and control based on the rigid, steep, and hierarchical policy making structure. It is an old and analog-style of the work process.

On the other hand, the contemporary way is based on the Smart paradigm. The Smart paradigm highlights the clear policy goal setting, effective policy making and analysis with quantitative and foresight tools and methodologies, new government reform with BPR(business reengineering process), and updating the legal framework. For the better work process, e-transformation based on BPR is very critical. The goal is to make a more slim, agile, and flexible policy making system with an aid of more smart and innovative technologies to make more open and transparent culture.

Figure 3-1 Traditional way & modern way

Traditional Way	Modern Way
Traditional Administration: • Command & Control • Rigid, Hierarchical Model • Bureaucracy • Analogue and Old Style	SMART Paradigm: • Clear policy Goal Setting • Effective Policy Making & Analysis (Regression Analysis, Policy Delphi & Scenario Planning, Foresight Methodologies) • New Government Reform • Business Process Reengineering New Work Process with E-Transformation: (Organizational structure, Technology innovation, Culture & Attitude change) • Updating Legal Framework

Effective Policy Making and Government 3.0

We are living in a more democratic society that people's participation and demands are increasing. Citizens have been requesting the correction of government failures and wanting more choices from the public service that suit their needs. They expect that the quality of public service should coequal with that of the private sector. As shown in the following Figure, the citizen, after reaching the basic expectations of material service, through the value-added service of customization and personalization, moves toward the best the top-level leading service of "Involve me, Inspire me, and Remember me!"

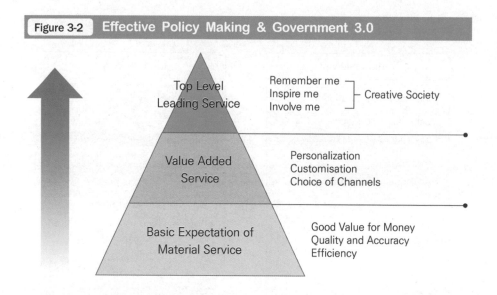

Figure 3-2 Effective Policy Making & Government 3.0

Therefore they are more sensitive about the cost and benefit of taxes they are paying, more critical about the bureaucratic and inefficient administration. As a result, they are demanding more competitive government with greater citizen satisfaction, which could be expected to be fully realized in Government 3.0.

Public Value Management Model and Government 3.0

Mark Moore(1995) presented the public value management model as the third generation governance model. If we call the bureaucratic government as the first-generation model, and the NPM(New Public Management) model as the second generation model, the PVM(Public Value Model) could be called as the third-generation model of governance or Government model 3.0. This PVM model emphasizes the public value compared to the market value emphasized by the NPM model(see Figure below)

In a Government 3.0, the PVM paradigm includes the following perspectives:

First, the public value of government 3.0 is the collective preference of all individuals of the nation, which might be derived from the process of deliberative democracy.

Second, the performance objective of government 3.0 is to consider the diverse aspects of satisfaction, outcome, trust, transparency, and accountability from the public services, rather than the mere consideration of input and output of the previous models.

Third, the accountability mechanism of government 3.0 highlights the active role of citizens. Citizens should play the role of monitoring or inspecting government, beyond the roles of just tax-payers or clients/customers as users.

Fourth, the service delivery system of government 3.0 highlights the public-private partnership or collaborative governance among the diverse stakeholders including government agencies, public enterprises, private companies, interest groups, or local communities.

| Figure 3-3 | Paradigm of Government 3.0 |

	Traditional Bureaucratic Model	New Public Management	Public Value Management
Public Interest	Defined by Politicians/ Government	Aggregation of Individual Preferences Demonstrated by Customer Choice	Individual and Public Preferences Derived from the Political Process of Deliberative Democracy
Performance Objective	Managing Inputs	Managing Inputs and Outputs	Multiple Objectives: ·Outputs ·Outcome ·Satisfaction ·Trust ·Transparency ·Accountability

	Traditional Bureaucratic Model	New Public Management	Public Value Management
Accountability Mechanism	Upwards through Department to Politicians and through them to Parliament	Upwards through Performance Contracts; Sometimes Outward to the Customers through Market Mechanisms	Multiple: ·Citizens as Inspector of Government ·Customers as users ·Taxpayers as funders
Public Service Delivering System	Bureaucracy Hierarchical System (Command & Control)	Private Sector or Special Agency (Market Mechanism)	Menu of Alternatives Selected Contextually (Government Agencies, Public Enterprises, Private Companies, Interest Groups, Local Community)
Public Service Ethos	Public Sector has a Monopoly on Service Ethos	Skeptical of Public Sector Ethos(Leads to Inefficiency and Empire Building) – Favors Customer Service by Market Mechanism	No One Ethos Always Appropriate. Public Good and Services, as a Community Resource, Should be Carefully Managed.
Role of Public Participation	Limited to Voting in Elections and Pressure on Elected Representatives	Limited Expressed only in the form of Customer Satisfaction	Crucial-multifaceted Stakeholders(Citizen, Customer/client, Taxpayer)
Goal of Government	Respond to Political Direction	Focusing on Performance Targets	Trust Building by Forming Network Governance Providing a Legal and Regulatory Framework Responding to Citizen by Guaranteeing Quality Services.

* Source: Revised from Mark Moore(1995); Kelly and Muers(2002).

Fifth, the public service ethos of government 3.0 is to avoid government monopoly or to think that no one ethos is always appropriate. Public goods and services, as a community resource, should be carefully managed.

Six, the role of public participation, therefore, should be multifaceted as a tax-payer, client, customer, or citizen.

Seven, the goal of government 3.0 should be the one formulating the new network governance to establish trust and social capital among the stakeholders by guaranteeing quality services responding to citizens and providing a legal and regulatory framework(Kelly and Muers, 2002).

Government 3.0 and e-Government 3.0

E-Government 3.0, based on the paradigm of Government 3.0, highlights the strategic setting and transformation by utilizing the Smart knowledge management of big data, sensor-based technologies, and semantic-based algorithm. If e-Government 1.0 emphasized the government's internal efficiency by using the concept of BPR, G2B, G2G, and G4C,e-Government 2.0 emphasizes the Open Platform of participation, sharing, open, and collective intelligence, highlighted by Web 2.0(see Table 9-1).

Korean Model of e-Government 3.0

Korean e-Government 3.0 evolved following prior models of e-Governments 1.0 and 2.0.

The first generation of e-Government, that is, e-Government 1.0 was from the late 1990s to 2002 in Korea when President Kim Dae-Jung government initially constructs the infrastructure of e-Government. Of course, these were possible by the efforts of the previous regimes such as the economic development of President Park Jung-Hee and among others.

In this period of e-Government 1.0, the Korean government established the basic infrastructure of administrative information networks and the information superhighway. Notably, the Kim Dae-Jung government established the special committee of e-Government, which was very helpful to set up a comprehensive and systematic blueprint of Korean e-Government at that time. Basically, in this period, e-Government1.0 tried to enhance effectiveness and efficiency by implementing government integrated e-Procurement system and the project of 'government for the citizen.' The major policy instruments used in this period is BPR, IRM, and ERP to enhance the public services of G2B, G2C, and G4C.

The second generation of Korean e-Government, that is, e-Government2.0 was from 2003 to 2012 when the Korean government had developed e-Government at the advanced stage of Web 2.0 of openness, participatory, and information sharing. People started to use and participated in the new online services such as the online banking system and 'Oasis'(http://oasis.seoul.go.kr) utilizing the advanced technology of Web 2.0. In this period of e-Government 2.0, the Korean government tried to enhance innovation and participation by enhancing the online services in which people could freely participate and suggest new policy ideas. In addition, the Government expanded the project of public information sharing and government information common utilization. The major policy instruments used in this period are Web 2.0 of open, participation, and collective intelligence.

The third generation of e-Government, that is, e-Government3.0 is from 2013 and it is in the current progress based on the development of the previous achievement of 1.0 and 2.0. It is the model attempted in the Korean President Park Geun-Hae government. E-Government 3.0 highlights strategic directional setting and transformation by utilizing the new smart technologies such as Big Data, Semantic Web based algorithm, RFID, and Sensor-based u-Technologies, and KMS system. It emphasizes "Do the Right Things" rather than "Do Things Right" and therefore it is not searching for mere efficiency but the right direction of national transformation or government reinvention. In this regard, the ideology aimed at this model 3.0 is trust, accountability, and reflexivity.

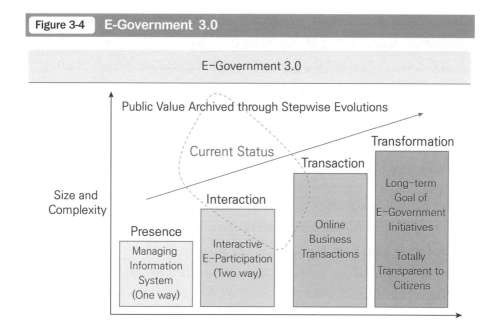

Figure 3-4   E-Government 3.0

The vision of e-Government 3.0 is to achieve a humanity-based society in which people's human dignity and quality of life are enhanced based on the democratic governance of transparency, accountability, and reflexivity.

To achieve this vision and goals, e-Government 3.0 requires the following policy strategies:

First, from the perspective of government as an institution, e-Government 3.0 requires the adoption of Smart technologies and strategies in transforming government by removing the silos and sectionalism. It emphasizes the need to upgrade the total intelligence of the nation by rearranging the information, knowledge, and resources scattered around the nation, thereby meeting the vision of the nation expressed by the people's happiness.

Second, from the perspective of public service, e-Government 3.0 emphasizes information sharing, openness, and collective intelligence.

Third, from the perspective of Big Data, e-Government 3.0 emphasizes the right decision-making and collaboration based on the systematic knowledge management of smart technologies and big data. It is an upgraded model to serve pre-emptive, forecasting, and customized services to each people, which is one-step developed beyond the just interactive services of e-Government 2.0.

Finally, to guarantee the above-mentioned services, the quality of system, service, and information that will lead towards trust and security should be satisfied first. That is, information security and protection of personal information are a very important foundation of the services.

In a nutshell, e-Government 3.0 is the advanced model of e-Government that could provide personal customized services or forecasting services utilizing big data and smart knowledge management technologies. Here, this model highlights the value of government services to meet people's happiness and therefore emphasizes the citizen as the main actor of democratic governance, not just a taxpayer or client as a user. Base on the spirit of open, participation, and network, people as a citizen is encouraged to participate and suggest new policy ideas to the democratic political processes by using new smart ICT technologies and Social Network Services.

▌ Effective Policy Making and Business Process Reengineering

Concept

The Business Process Reengineering (BPR)first introduced by Michael Hammer and immediately followed by P. Drucker, M. Porter, and E. Deming denotes a fundamental redesign of the business process. The philosophy of BPR is based on the innovative thoughts that if we want to survive in the competition, it requires a fundamental rethinking from the basic way of doing business.

BPR is defined to rebuild the system by changing the people, process, and technology utilizing the smart information technology that fundamentally reconsiders the traditional way in all parts of the business process.

Features

BPR has the following features:

First, BPR is an innovation. It redesigns the internal business process to enhance innovation, thus increasing customer satisfaction. Time-saving, cost reduction and downsizing is an associated effect.

Second, BPR pursues a zero-based approach. It requires a fundamental reconsideration in all the ways of the existing approach.

Third, BPR focuses on the process. It makes business processes innovative and faster enhancement of customer satisfaction.

Fourth, BPR pursues innovative goal-setting, say, at least 30%, or from 50% to 100% increase of goal achievement.

Finally, BPR actively utilizes the new information technology. It utilizes smart ICT as a tool of innovation, standardizes the results of innovation, and proliferated them to the other parts of the organization.

Critical Success Factors

The critical success factors for BPR include three key elements: People, Process, and Information technology.

1) People

If a person does not change, we can never expect the successful result of BPR. Consider the following strategies:

- Change process involving key stakeholders and internal workflow
- Eliminate duplicate or redundant business processes
- Redesign the business process from the viewpoint of customer satisfaction
- Perform organizational restructuring from the process efficiency
- Review laws and regulatory framework to support the above activities

2) Process

Reengineering the business process is the key to successful BPR. Consider the following strategies:

- Focus on the time-consuming process
- Give attention on paperwork processes involving several departments
- Distinguish high-value, low-value-added process
- Distinguish high-risk, low-risk process
- Distinguish high-accountability, low-accountability process
- Remove unnecessary, duplicate, and redundant non-value-added work
- Readjust business range according to the level of risk
- Reengineer business process for performing work with high accountability

3) Technology

Information technology is the key instrument for successful BPR. Consider the following strategies:

- Establish the smart ICT infrastructure for innovating and shortening business process
- Redesign and integrate business process by utilizing ICT to speed up and to prevent from disconnected knowledge flow
- Establish an IRM system for knowledge creation and utilization
- Establish an integrated DB or DW system for knowledge accumulation and sharing
- Establish overall-company, ERP system for knowledge learning and proliferation by including customers and suppliers, or citizen, stakeholders, and other related agencies

Strategy

To operate BPR properly, we should take note of the following stages in establishing BPR:

1) Strategic Planning Stage

In this stage, the strategies, plans, and a specific schedule of future activities of BPR are developed. Here, establish project strategy, define project success factors, construct the project infrastructure, plan detailed schedule, BPR initiated meetings, training and education, and basic benchmarking activity, are performed.

2) Diagnostic Stage

In this stage, the authorized agency tries to diagnose the status of the organization by analyzing its strength and weakness, opportunities, and threats. Based on the analysis, the organization performs the workshops and brainstorming activities on how to remedy the problematic points of the process. In the workshop, select the target process, job analysis, discuss how to remove and readjust unnecessary, duplicate, and redundant processes, are performed.

3) Re-design Stage

In this stage, the agency redesigns the future process analyzed by the previous steps. Here, re-design the future process; establish the action plan and action-resolution meetings are performed.

4) Implementation Stage

In this stage, the agency implements the concrete actions taking into account the suggestions and recommendations made during the redesign stage. Here, the reengineering, reform activities, monitoring and feedback, standardization, selects the best practice, and wrapping up the session, are performed.

5) Maintenance and Update Stage

In this stage, the agency concludes the first step of BPR and establishes the plan for the next step of the second stage of BPR for the continuous innovation of the organizational process.

Crucial Questions

For the effective BPR, you should consider 6-W questions, Why, What, Where, How, Who, and When. The six crucial questions are as follows:

- Understand why the business must change via the drivers
- Connect what are the benefits to the business processes
- Understand where the changes will happen in the organization units
- Determine how to make the changes via projects
- Identify who are the stakeholders
- When changes will be implemented on the right timeline

Figure 3-5	The Benefits Dependency Network/BPM

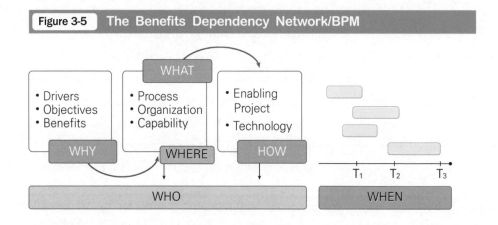

How to achieve e-Transformation using BPR

For the effective e-Transformation, we need to utilize BPR(BPM or Benefits Dependency Network in a broader sense). The critical steps are as follows:

Stage 1: Mapping Existing Process

In stage 1, you need to develop the framework and produce a flowchart.

Stage 2: Define Aspired End-state

In stage 2, you need to analyze the process and capacities of your agency and provide a clear image on the result of redesign.

Stage 3: GAP Analysis

In stage 3, you need to compare between the aspired End-state (to-be) and the Current-state (as-is).

And highlight the functions that should be eliminated or reinforced.

Stage 4: Design Action Plan

In stage 4, you need to assign clear responsibilities. Finally, determine the Change Control Mechanism with special attention to the People's Attitude Change within the organization.

Figure 3-6 How to Achieve e-Transformation using BPR?

Stage 1:
Mapping Existing
Process

Develop the
Framework
Produce a
Flowchart

Stage 2:
Define Aspired
End-state

Analysis of the Process
and Capacities.
Provide Clear Image
for what the Redesign
can result in

Stage 3:
GAP Analysis

Comparison between
the aspired End-state
and the Current-state.
Highlight the functions that
should be Eliminated
or Reinforced

Stage 4:
Design Action Plan
Assign Clear
Responsibilities

Determine Change Control
Mechanism
with Special
Attention on
the People's
Attitude Change

BPR and Smart E-Government

When we apply BPR to government organizations, much more careful considerations should be paid. As BPR is to highlight the rapid changes of business processes across the organizations, it makes the risk of failure greater. Especially the characteristics of the public administrative organizations are status-quo oriented and risk-aversive.

In addition, the government organization is not like the business organization as it should take into account the diverse values of the democratic regime such as democracy, equality, fairness, legitimacy, and accountability. It is unlike that private organization mainly considers mere efficiency and profitability. This had been the reason that BPR could not be easily adopted in government organizations.

However, things have been changed. The national governance model has been changed searching for a more competitive, productive, and customer-oriented one. Especially with the adoption of e-Government and knowledge government, the main issues of government innovation become more similar to the ones of entrepreneurial business organizations. For example, e-Government now concerns such issues like, how to kindly treat citizen as a customer or client, how to transparently involve them to the policy processes, how to utilize smart ICT technologies to cut down the red tapes and unnecessary processes to conveniently provide them with one-stop, any-stop, or non-stop services, which would lead to enhancing the people's quality of life and people's happiness.

Nevertheless, we should pay careful attention when we apply BPR to government organizations. Special attention should include the following points:

(1) Do not consider only the narrow economic values like efficiency.
(2) Consider public interest by accommodating a variety of values like democracy and equity.
(3) Consider public interest by accommodating a variety of stakeholders.
(4) Consider the modest strategies. It is possible that BPR damages public value and interest.

Effective Policy Making and Government 4.0

We are living in a more turbulent society that is characterized by volatile, uncertainty, complexity, and ambiguity (VUCA) of the 4th Industrial Revolution (IR). As globalization and the 4th IR deepens in this contemporary age, uncertainty and complexity of wicked problems are ever heightened. Under this age of turbulence, innovation is crucial to achieving the transformation of governance under society 4.0. To achieve innovation and transformation, effective policy making is indispensable.

Recently, Harvard John F. Kennedy School of Government established a new policy research center named Future Society (see Figure below). Echoing J. F. Kennedy's famous vision, "on the edge of a new frontier," and from the perception that new technologies in the 4[th]IR, the research think-tank embarked on the new research about NBIC(Nano, Bio, Information, Cognitive brain science) and a new creative policy initiatives. They are stressing that we need a new vision of effective policy making under the vision of society 4.0, as our society is facing an array of crucial ethical questions and policy choices.

Figure 3-7　Harvard JFK School NBIC

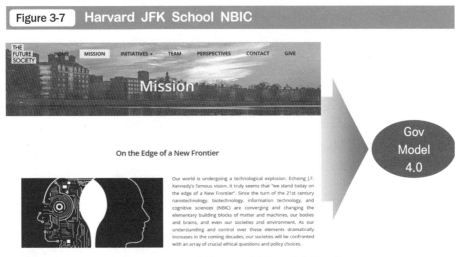

- NBIC(Nano, Bio, Information, Cognitive Tech) Exponential Growth & Development
- Coping with the Fundamental Ethical Challenges
- Suggesting the New Paradigm of Policy Initiatives

Effective Policy Making: New Challenges

The government model has evolved through a different stage, namely Government 1.0, 2.0, 3.0, and now we are facing a new governance model. Government 1.0 was a traditional way of administration based on Max Weber's Bureaucratic model. Government 2.0 was a market approach of administration based on New Public Management. Government 3.0 was a value approach of administration based on Mark Moore's Public Value Model. Now, as discussed in this chapter, we are facing a new and different turn, more chaotic and turbulent society, characterized by volatility, uncertainty, complexity, and ambiguity. We are not only witnessing a new developments in technology but also a facing global pandemic like COVID-19 that is greatly changing our social life. Such a swirl of revolutionary challenges requires an unsullied evaluation of the existing governance model and its operating system. Industry 4.0, artificial intelligence, NBIC, and the new global health crisis with other social and natural disasters are ahead of us at a heightened uncertainty. We have to consider seriously the new agile governance model with a more responsible and responsive leadership.

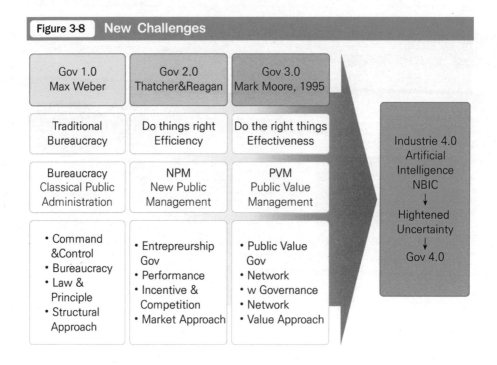

Figure 3-8 **New Challenges**

Gov 1.0 Max Weber	Gov 2.0 Thatcher&Reagan	Gov 3.0 Mark Moore, 1995	
Traditional Bureaucracy	Do things right Efficiency	Do the right things Effectiveness	Industrie 4.0 Artificial Intelligence NBIC ↓ Hightened Uncertainty ↓ Gov 4.0
Bureaucracy Classical Public Administration	NPM New Public Management	PVM Public Value Management	
• Command &Control • Bureaucracy • Law & Principle • Structural Approach	• Entrepreurship Gov • Performance • Incentive & Competition • Market Approach	• Public Value Gov • Network • w Governance • Network • Value Approach	

Smart Policy Framework: New Vision

Smart Governance 4.0 highlights a new vision of a strong and great nation with effective policy making in which government, market corporates, and NGOs are collaboratively networking with a trustful and mature manner. It also highlights government accountability more than ever before as we vividly saw in the crisis of COVID-19. In this sense, the new framework seeks to clarify government's public value more clearly. Based on the smart e-government technology and more predictive policy making using foresight techniques, its tools and methodologies, the new framework should make more efforts to meet ever the growing people's expectations of not just delivering services but to provide public services more efficiently, effectively, agile and responsive way. They are asking "remember me, involve me, and inspire me."

Figure 3-9	New Vision

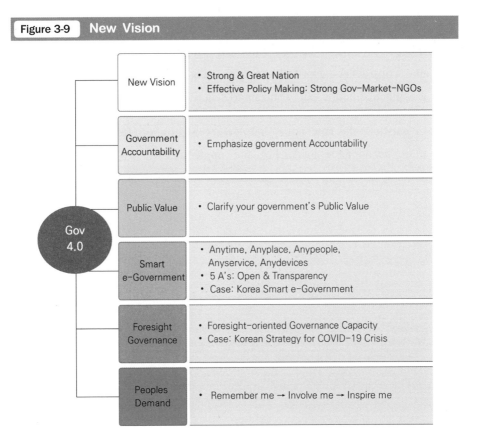

New Vision
- Strong & Great Nation
- Effective Policy Making: Strong Gov-Market-NGOs

Government Accountability
- Emphasize government Accountability

Public Value
- Clarify your government's Public Value

Gov 4.0

Smart e-Government
- Anytime, Anyplace, Anypeople, Anyservice, Anydevices
- 5 A's: Open & Transparency
- Case: Korea Smart e-Government

Foresight Governance
- Foresight-oriented Governance Capacity
- Case: Korean Strategy for COVID-19 Crisis

Peoples Demand
- Remember me → Involve me → Inspire me

Summary and Conclusion: Smart Policy Framework 4.0

This chapter highlighted Smart Policy Framework 4.0 with a review of previous governance models.

The Smart Policy Framework 4.0 highlights human dignity and public value in a more speedy, ethical, and efficient way. The goal in this framework is to make big data and evidence-based creative governance with effective policy making. The strategy is three-fold: speed, wisdom, and fusion.

First, as for speed, the new framework emphasizes the new capacity building to make quick responses to the new social problems.

Second, as for wisdom, the new framework emphasizes the responsive and responsible leadership by providing pre-emptive responsive and smart system.

Finally, as for fusion, the new framework emphasizes a more interdisciplinary and consilience approach to providing new services with a more strengthened public safety and smart security infrastructure.

In a nutshell, the new policy framework highlights effective policymaking with more accountable leadership and implementation. Also, it is an agile governance system using smart e-government technologies and digital capacities.

Figure 3-10	SMART FRAMEWORK 4.0

VISION	Human Dignity & Public Value

Goal	Big Data and Intelligence Based Creative Governance: Effective Policy Making

STRATEGY	Speed	Wisdom	Fusion

- Effective Policy Making: Quick Response to the Social Problems
- Evidence-Based Intelligence Governance

1. Speed: Speedy Problem Solving
2. Wisdom: Responsive and Responsible Leadership
   Pre-emptive Response and Re-education, Government Accountability
3. Fusion: Strengthening Public Safety and Security Infrastructure

Key Point!

1. The Structural Approach to Effective Policy Making
To demonstrate the paradigm of effective policymaking, we need to understand the administrative, policy, and governance model looking at both the traditional and contemporary approaches and delving on Governance transformation from the so-called Governance 1.0, 2.0, 3.0, and 4.0.

2. Effective Policy Making and Government 3.0
▶ After reaching the basic expectations of material service, through the value-added service of customization and personalization, the citizen expectation moves toward the best the top-level leading service of "Involve me, Inspire me, and Remember me!"

3. Effective Policy Making and Government 4.0
▶ Harvard John F. Kennedy School of Government recently established a new policy research center named Future Society and embarked on the new research about NBIC(Nano, Bio, Information, Cognitive brain science) and a new creative policy initiatives.

▶ They are stressing that we need a new vision of effective policy making under the vision of society 4.0, as our society is facing an array of crucial ethical questions and policy choices.

4. Smart Policy Framework 4.0
▶ Smart policy framework 4.0 highlights human dignity and public value in a more speedy, ethical, and efficient way.

▶ The goal in this framework is to make big data and evidence-based creative governance with effective policy making.

▶ The strategy is three-fold: speed, wisdom, and fusion.

▶ Finally, for considering Smart Policy Framework 4.0, we need to take into account the following new challenges & new vision.

New Challenges

▶ We are not only witnessing a new developments in technology but also a facing global pandemic like COVID-19 that is greatly changing our social life. Such a swirl of revolutionary challenges requires an unsullied evaluation of the existing governance model and its operating system.

▶ Industry 4.0, artificial intelligence, NBIC, and the new virus Crises with other social disasters approaching us as a heightened uncertainty, we have to consider seriously the new agile governance model with a more responsible and responsive leadership.

New Vision

▶ Smart Governance 4.0 highlights a new vision of a strong and great nation with effective policy making in which government, market corporates, and NGOs are collaboratively networking with a trustful and mature manner.

▶ It also highlights government accountability more than ever before as we vividly saw in the crisis of COVID-19.

▶ In a nutshell, the new policy framework highlights effective policy making and an agile governance system using smart e-government technologies and digital capacities.

Figure 3-11 Discussion Question: Smart Policy Framework

Effective
Policy
Making

- What is Smart Policy Framework 4.0?
- What is it different from the previous model 1.0, 2.0, and 3.0?
- What is BPR?
- What are the stages of e-Transformation?
- Discuss about Harvard model of NBIC, What would that be?
- What kind of implications and lessons we should get from the Harvard Model?

PART 2

POLICY PARADIGM & MODELS

Chapter 4

POLICY PARADIGM
The Conceptual Approach for Effective Policy Making

Policy paradigm is the foundation for policy science. To learn effective policy making, we have to understand the basic concepts and theories of policy science.

✎ ››› Objectives

The purpose of this chapter is to elucidate the conceptual approach for effective policy making.

First, for the conceptual components, it will highlight the concept, future, critical element, successful steps, performance criteria, and policy target group.

Second, for the successful conditions, it will highlight three aspects: policy variable, policy stage, and policy types

Finally, it will present the comprehensive design for effective policy making and the final criteria for policy success.

The Conceptual Approach to Effective Policy Making: Concept, Critical Elements, and Criteria

Concept

Policy is a government dictation to make a desirable state in your society. For this purpose, the government should use scientific policy instruments to achieve national vision and goals.

Figure 4-1 The Concept of Policy

• Definition

> Policy is a government dictation to make a desirable state in your society. For this purpose, government should use the scientific policy instruments to achieve national vision and goals.

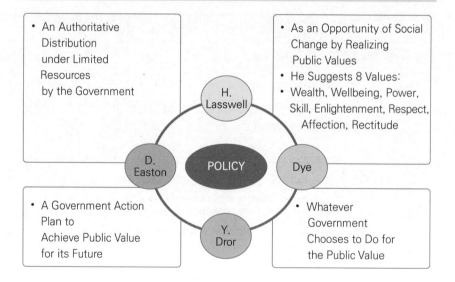

• An Authoritative Distribution under Limited Resources by the Government

• As an Opportunity of Social Change by Realizing Public Values
• He Suggests 8 Values:
• Wealth, Wellbeing, Power, Skill, Enlightenment, Respect, Affection, Rectitude

H. Lasswell

D. Easton

POLICY

Dye

Y. Dror

• A Government Action Plan to Achieve Public Value for its Future

• Whatever Government Chooses to Do for the Public Value

For instance, H. Lasswell, the founder of policy science, defined public policy as an Opportunity of Social Change in the near future by Realizing Public Values. He suggested the eight crucial public values: Wealth, Wellbeing, Power, Skill, Enlightenment, Respect, Affection, and Rectitude. From another angle, Y. Dror, defined public policy as a Government Action Plan to Achieve Public Value for its Future. We can readily notice that these important scholars in this field especially emphasize the value of the future.

Future

For effective policy making, we need to take special attention to the future. There are at least three important futures: Probable, Desirable, and Potential. A probable future is a future that probably happens if the government does not intervene with a special action. That is the situation that the current social problems would still exist in that future. That is why we need a special action, called effective policy making by the government to solve the existing problems within society, hopefully with foresight technologies. Then the tendency was broken and the fundamental problems would be solved, and we could achieve the vision of a strong and great nation. We call this desirable situation achieving great vision as the desirable future. Between this desirable future and probable future, there are many potential futures as shown in the below diagram.

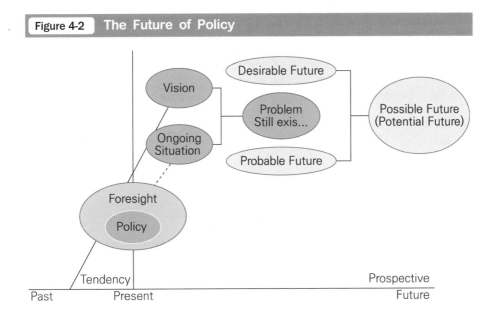

Figure 4-2 The Future of Policy

Critical Elements

Effective policy making has three critical components: goal, instrument, and target group.

First, the goal, the desired state that the government attempts to realize, should be clear and consistent, targeting the creative future vision of the nation.

Second, the instrument, a means to achieve the goal, should be derived from the scientific analysis and foresight(we will discuss its methodologies in the Policy Analysis section).

Finally, the target group, customer or client or people in a broad sense, should be treated in a very responsible and responsive way to achieve human dignity or the policy science of democracy. It should be agile and speedy delivery in an accountable and transparent manner. To do that, the government should produce a feasible action plan.

Figure 4-3	The Critical Elements of Effective Policy Making

Critical Elements

Goal	• A Desired State that Government attempts to realize • Creative, Future-oriented goal
Instrument	• Means to achieve its goal • Instruments should derive based on scientific analysis & foresight
Target Group	• Responsive and Responsible • Agile and Accountable • Effective policy making should produce a feasible action plan
Effective Policy Making	• Effective policy making should remember goal, instrument, and target group.

Successful Steps

Effective policy making needs to follow three critical steps with three standards: causal validity, realistic feasibility, and normative standards such as reflexivity.

1) **Causal Validity**: It means a valid Causal Relationship between policy goal and instrument. It should be effective and efficient. To ensure this dimension, we will do a cost-benefit analysis, cost-effective analysis, among others.

2) **Realistic Feasibility**: It means six feasibility criteria: political, financial, social, administrative, legal, technical feasibility.

3) **Normative Standard**: Reflexivity: It is a normative standard. We call it the reflexivity dimension. It is the highest vision of public policy, ultimately realizing human dignity. It has two levels, one with the individual for the self-realization of each individual, the other with the community for realizing a trustful & matured society.

| Figure 4-4 | The Successful Steps of Effective Policy Making |

Criteria

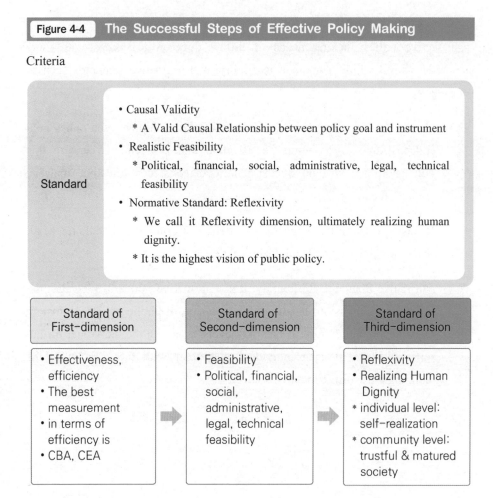

Standard

- Causal Validity
    - * A Valid Causal Relationship between policy goal and instrument
- Realistic Feasibility
    - * Political, financial, social, administrative, legal, technical feasibility
- Normative Standard: Reflexivity
    - * We call it Reflexivity dimension, ultimately realizing human dignity.
    - * It is the highest vision of public policy.

Standard of First-dimension	Standard of Second-dimension	Standard of Third-dimension
• Effectiveness, efficiency • The best measurement • in terms of efficiency is • CBA, CEA	• Feasibility • Political, financial, social, administrative, legal, technical feasibility	• Reflexivity • Realizing Human Dignity * individual level: self-realization * community level: trustful & matured society

Performance Criteria

Effective policy making will be assessed by the three different performance criteria: output, outcome, and impact.

1) **Output**: It is the first and tangible results in the short term. It can be expressed by numbers and can be quantifiable. In education policy, it is the number of students who graduate from high school.

2) **Outcome**: It is the second and policy effect in the middle-range term. It is an intermediate-term effect. In education policy, it is the education performance or real capacity from education, not just the number of

graduates.

3) **Impact**: It is the third and Long-term effect on society. In education policy, for instance, it is the measurement for a trustful and mature citizen from the education effect.

Figure 4-5 **Three Performance**

Policy Output, Outcome, Impact: don't misunderstand output & outcome!

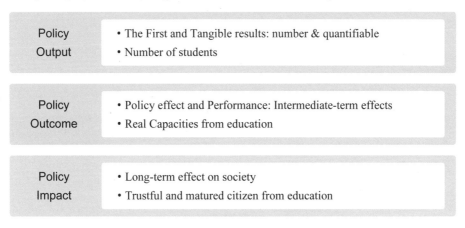

Policy Output	• The First and Tangible results: number & quantifiable • Number of students
Policy Outcome	• Policy effect and Performance: Intermediate-term effects • Real Capacities from education
Policy Impact	• Long-term effect on society • Trustful and matured citizen from education

Policy Target Group

Goal, instrument, Target group are the three critical components for effective policymaking, as mentioned. For effective policy making, we need to understand there are two types of the target group, one with the beneficiary group, and the other with the sacrificing group. Also, for the final policy success, we need to understand four important variables affecting the policy success: size, level, past experiences, and behaviors to be changed.

1) **Size**: The smaller size of the target group is easier to be implemented. Therefore, it is more likely to lead to policy success compared to the large size of the target group.

2) **Level**: The more beneficiary groups and the less sacrificing groups are

more likely to lead to policy success.

3) **Experience**: The policy with a favorable experience is more likely to lead to policy success.

4) **Behavior to be changed**: The simpler and smaller form of change from the initiation of a new policy is more likely to lead to policy success.

Figure 4-6   Target Group of   Effective Policy Making

Policy Target Groups

Successful Conditions for Effective Policy Making: Policy Variable, Policy Stage, and Policy Types

The successful conditions for effective policy making, we need to analyze policy variables, policy stages, and policy types.

1) **Variable**: The critical policy variables are: Public officials, Structure, and Environment. For public officials, we need to cultivate more capable and dedicated capacity building. For structure, we need a more agile, speedy, and flexible organizational structure to make more fast, agile, and responsive delivery system. For the environment, we need to emphasize the sensitive learning of the government, always awakened and aware of the external signals from the environment. This environment could be the whole people within the nation or international political-economic situation from abroad.

| Figure 4-7 | Three Key Variables of Policy System |

Three Key Variables

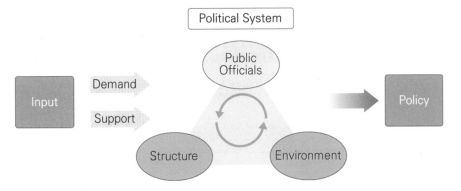

2) **Stage**: The critical policy stages are: Agenda setting, Policymaking, Policy Analysis, Implementation, Evaluation, and Change.

3) **Types**: The critical policy types are: regulation, redistribution, distribution,

and constitution policy. It is important to understand the typologies of the policy when approaching as it has some different features respectively. For example, people are generally very sensitive to the regulation policy, especially for regulated people. This regulation policy has two types, again: protective regulation and competitive regulation. The protective regulation policy is to protect people from negative effects Such as regulating pollution to protect the air quality of the business or private sector activities for public interests. And the competitive regulation policy is to exclusively allow for a service provider to the chosen providers, for example, allocating Airplane lines or DMV, Smart Mobile Industries. It is an open competition for new business companies; once adopted, it will make a huge amount of money. But because of its public interest like broadcasting or airplanes, the government will regulate even after it is adopted.

| Figure 4-8 | Effective Policy Making |

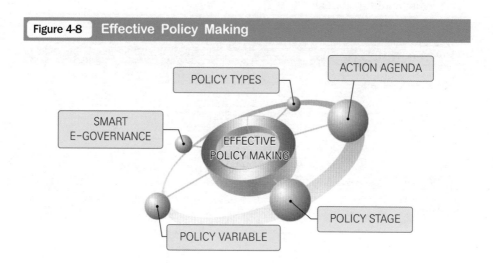

Successful Conditions for Effective Policy Making: Comprehensive Design

The successful conditions for effective policy making, we need to elucidate the comprehensive design, shown in the below. The vision is to make a strong and great nation. To accomplish this great vision, we need governance innovation with three-dimensional criteria: efficiency, democracy, and reflexivity. And to achieve this goal, we need policy innovation by analyzing three components: variable, stage, and typology. As the core, there exists the analytical framework of effective policymaking.

Figure 4-9 Strong & Great Nation

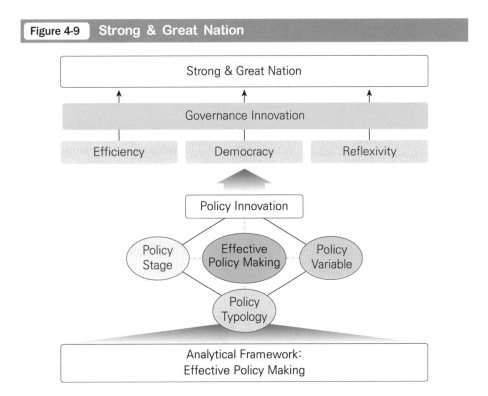

Summary and Conclusions

In this chapter, we have discussed many critical elements for effective policy making. We reviewed concepts, critical elements, successful steps, performance criteria, and comprehensive design. Before closing this chapter, we finally recapitalize the fundamental conditions for policy success. The fundamental items are four dimensions: priority, desirability feasibility, and human resources.

1) **Goal: Priority**: The goal of policy should be clear and consistent.

2) **Instrument: Desirability & Feasibility**: The instrument of policy should be desirable and feasible. The desirability has six elements: effectiveness, efficiency, equity, responsiveness, adequacy, and appropriateness. The feasibility has again six-element: political, financial, social, administrative, legal, and technical.

3) **Target Group: Human Resources**: The target group should be managed strategically. For this purpose, we need to cultivate capacity building for human resources in developing countries. It should have two dimensions: capacity and dedications. The first one is related to ability and the second one is related to attitude change.

| Figure 4-10 | POLICY SUCCESS |

Key Point!

1. The Conceptual Approach to Effective Policy Making

   Concept

   ▶ Policy is a government dictation to make a desirable state in your society. For this purpose, the government should use scientific policy instruments to achieve national vision and goals.

   Critical Elements

   ▶ Effective policy making has three critical components: goal, instrument, and target group.

   Successful Steps

   ▶ Effective policy making needs to follow three critical steps with three standards: causal validity, realistic feasibility, and normative standards such as reflexivity.

   1) Causal Validity: It means a valid Causal Relationship between policy goal and instrument. It should be effective and efficient.
   2) Realistic Feasibility: It means six feasibility criteria: political, financial, social, administrative, legal, technical feasibility.
   3) Normative Standard: Reflexivity: It is a normative standard. We call it the reflexivity dimension. It is the highest vision of public policy, ultimately realizing human dignity.

2. Successful Conditions for Effective Policy Making

   ▶ The successful conditions for effective policy making, we need to analyze policy variables, policy stages, and policy types.
   1) Variable: The critical policy variables are: Public officials, Structure,

and Environment.

2) Stage: The critical policy stages are: Agenda setting, Policymaking, Policy Analysis, Implementation, Evaluation, and Change.

3) Types: The critical policy types are: regulation, redistribution, distribution, and constitution policy. It is important to understand the typologies of the policy when approaching as it has some different features respectively.

3. Successful Conditions of Comprehensive Design

▶ The successful conditions for effective policy making, we need to elucidate the comprehensive design, shown in the below. The vision is to make a strong and great nation. To accomplish this great vision, we need governance innovation with three-dimensional criteria: efficiency, democracy, and reflexivity. And to achieve this goal, we need policy innovation by analyzing three components: variable, stage, and typology. At the core, there exists the analytical framework of effective policymaking.

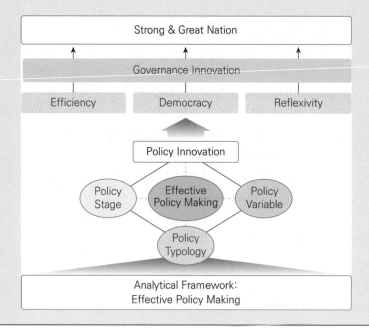

Figure 4-11	Discussion Question: Policy Paradigm

Effective Policy Making	• What are the three critical elements for effective policy making? • What are the four conditions of successful target group management? • What are the three criteria and dimensions of efficiency, democracy, and reflexivity? • What are the successful steps to proceeding those three dimensions?

Chapter 5

POLICY MODEL

The Policy Model Approach for Effective Policy Making

Policy model is the key to Policy Science. And the policy model is an artifact of real society. Therefore to elucidate the crucial policy models is to understand effective policy making.

✎ ››› Objectives

The purpose of this chapter is to elucidate the policy model approach for effective policymaking. The policy model, in this chapter, will review the policy making model, agenda-setting model, policy change model, and policy process model.

First, for the policy making model, it will highlight the rational model, satisfying model, incremental model, mixed-scanning, optimal model, garbage can, policy stream, and Allison model among others.

Second, for the agenda-setting model, it will highlight the mobilization model, external initiative model, and internal bureaucracy model.

Third, for the policy change model, it will highlight the Hofferbert model, the Sabatier model, the Mucciaroni model, the Kingdon model, and Hall model.

Finally, for the policy process model, it will highlight the Elite model, Pluralism model, Sub Government model, and Issue Network model.

Policy Making Model

Definition

Policymaking is a series of government decision making to set the cornerstone for the future of the nation. Also, it is the key to effective policy making as apparent in the name.

When discussing the policy making model, it is important to know the two aspects: positive and normative. The positive aspect asks the question, like, "what is the most realistic model empirically explaining the current situation of the policymaking process?" The normative aspect asks the question of "what is the most desirable model?"

The criteria or driving force of policymaking is:
1) public value
2) loyalty
3) local benefits such as the interests of the local electorate, and
4) national opinion

The features of policy making are
1) conflicts among many stakeholders
2) dynamic process
3) future-oriented, and
4) value-oriented as it is bound for human dignity, or to make a strong and great national innovation if you prefer.

Figure 5-1 Policy Making Model

Definition of Policy Making

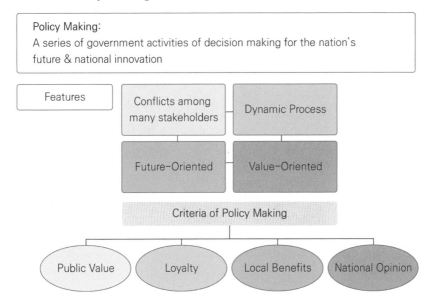

Policy Making:
A series of government activities of decision making for the nation's future & national innovation

Features

Conflicts among many stakeholders

Dynamic Process

Future-Oriented

Value-Oriented

Criteria of Policy Making

Public Value

Loyalty

Local Benefits

National Opinion

Steps

The steps of effective policy making are:

1) problem definition and goal setting

2) prioritizing between policy goals

3) development and plan of policy alternatives

4) future foresight and comparative evaluation of alternative results, and

5) choosing the best alternatives

Figure 5-2 Steps of Effective Policy Making

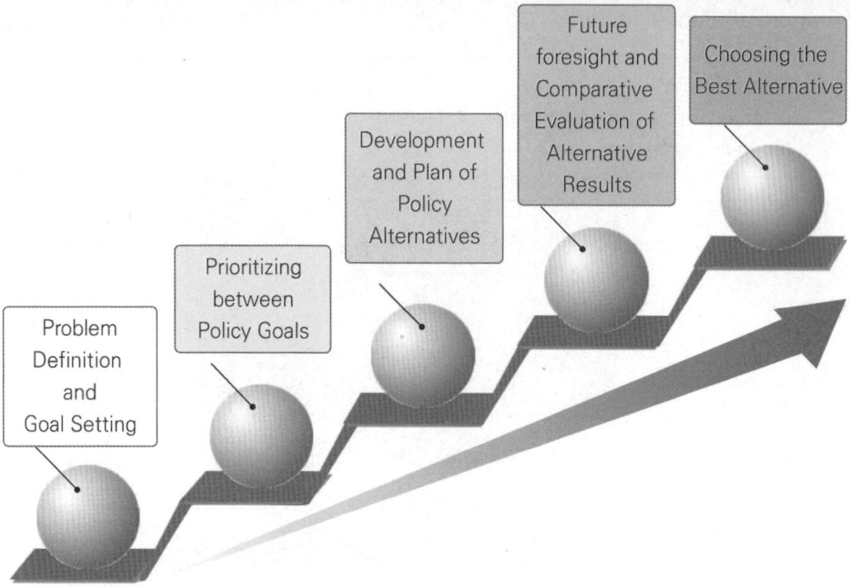

Typology

We will discuss the rational model, satisfying model, incremental model, mixed-scanning, optimal model, garbage can, policy stream, and Allison model among others.

Rational Model

Rational Model is an economic model based on human reason vs rationality. Neo Classical economists assumed the complete rationality such as

1) Complete Understanding of the Problem
2) Precisely Define the Goal
3) Identification of All Alternatives
4) Sufficient Resources, and
5) Choosing the best Optimal Option.

So, normatively appealing, but it has some misunderstanding of human capacity as a human being has a limited cognitive capacity with limited time and information. Oftentimes, it is hard to comprehend all the complex nature of policy & its uncertainty. For this very reason, we should consider the second model, a satisfying model.

Satisfying Model

Satisfying Model is suggested by H. Simon who criticized the limitations of Rational Models. By suggesting limited cognitive rationality, called a Bounded Rationality, H. Simon argued that people or organization chooses the satisficing alternatives rather than the best option because of cognitive limitations. With these theoretical contributions, he earned a Novel Prize. H. Simon set the cornerstones to behavioral economics which is one of the hot topics recently.

Incremental Model

An incremental model is suggested by Lindblom & Widavsky who argued that making a gradual & partial change is better. It is the model based on organization and budget rationality. Disjointed and sequential innovation makes sense to the plural and liberal democracy in the advanced nations but has a severe limitation for the developing countries as they should pursue total innovation with a limited time framework.

| Figure 5-3 | Policy Making Model |

Types of policy making model

Division	Rational Model	Satisfying Model	Incremental Model
Significance	• Economic Model based on Human Reason &Rationality	• H. Simon: Criticized the limitations of Rational Models	• Lindblom &Widavsky: • Making a Gradual &Partial Change is the better • Disjointed and Sequential improvement • Organization and Budget Rationality
Content	• Assume Complete Rationality: 1) Complete Understanding of the Problem 2) Precisely Define the Goal 3) Identification of All Alternatives 4) Sufficient Resources 5) Choosing the best Optimal Option	• Limited Cognitive Rationality (Bounded Rationality) • Choice of Satisficing Alternatives (rather than the Best Criteria)	• Can be Applied better at the plural &liberal democracy • Harmful for the total Innovation
Criticism	• Limitations of Human Capacity • Incomplete Information and Time limit • Complex nature of policy &uncertainty	• Theoretical Contributions to Empirical analysis, Novel Laureate • Satisficing choices are overly Subjective	• Lack of Ideal Vision of Effective Policy Making

Mixed Scanning Model

Mixed Scanning model is suggested by A. Etzioni who argued that it is not ideal to just adopt one of the Rational Models or the Incremental Model. By emphasizing that the fundamental decision and detailed decision should be approached differently, the fundamental decision should be approached by the

Rational Model and the detailed decision should be approached by the Incremental Model. The fundamental decision is called Societal Guidance System, or National Innovation Roadmap. It is like two lenses are needed for accurate weather forecasting, the Hubble for a long distance with a wide range, the Micro for a short distance with a detailed range.

Optimal Model

The optimal model is suggested Y. Dror who criticized the Incremental Model. He also criticized the Rational Model saying that only economic efficiency is not enough. Rather he highlighted the Super-rationality by emphasizing the importance of systematic learning, originality, and creativity. Therefore, he argued for a new capacity building to improve effective policy making capacity by emphasizing to cultivate insight, intuition, and inspirational policymaking.

Y. Dror, age of 91, still actively researching these issues. He emphasizes the National Policy Decision Strategy with a Meta Policy Making. Meta Policy Making is policy making for policymaking. Before actual policymaking, we may need a total meta-level policy making such as what kind of decision making we need, what about time frameworks with appropriated resources, and staff members. Also, importantly, we need to ask ourselves, what kind of strategies we may adopt:

1) radical or incremental

2) innovative or conservative

3) risk-taking or risk avoided, and finally

4) long term or short term

Figure 5-4	Policy Making Model

Types of Policy Model

Division	Mixed Scanning Model	Optimal Model
Featured content	• A. Etzioni: Argued that it is not ideal to jest adopt one of the Rational Model or the Incremental Model. • Fundamental decision and Detailed decision should be approached differently. • Fundamental decision is called Societal Guidance System, or National Innovation Roadmap.	• Y. Dror: Emerged as a critique of the Incremental Model - Also Criticized the Rational model emphasizing only economic efficiency - Rather he emphasized the Super-rationality by highlighting the importance of systematic learning, originality, and creativity. - New HRD Capacity Building to improve effective policy making capacity by cultivating insight, intuition and inspirational policy making. - Innovative vs conservative - Radical vs incremental - Risk Taking vs Risk Avoided - Long-term vs Short-term Strategy
Strength	• Realization of Ideals of Rational Model while Overcoming the Conservativeness of the Incremental Model	• Emphasis on National Policy Decision Strategy (Mega-policy Making) • Mega-policy Making Policy Making Post-policy Making
Criticism	• Merely a Mixture of Basic Models	• Specific criteria for super-rationality is unclear

Garbage Can Model

Garbage Can model is suggested by J. March and J. Olsen who characterized the policy decision situation that is made in a very weak and confused state of cohesion. Like a garbage can, in which we throw papers, can, or food-leftover, in the garbage can, policy making is made out with the coincident joint of problem, solution, participants, and opportunity. These situations are based on the premise of

1) unclear preferences

2) an unclear causal relationship, and

3) passive and inactive participants

The examples are the University's Decision making or some of the North European countries like Norway, Finland, or Sweden.

Figure 5-5	Policy Making Model

Garbage Can Model

Characteristics of Policy Decisions that are made in a very weak and confused state of Cohesion
(J. March, J. Olsen)
Ex) University Decision making, Norway, Finland, or Sweden Cultures

Basic Premise

Unclear Preference	Unclear Technology (Causal Relationship)	Inactive Participants

Four Element

Problem	Solution (Alternatives)	Participants	Opportunity

Policy Stream Model

The Policy Stream model is suggested by J. Kingdon who wrote "Agendas, Alternatives, and Public Policies(1984)." He suggested three streams independently flow: problem, policy, and politics. He reframed the Garbage Can model from the four events(problem, policy, participants, and opportunity) to the three streams(problem, policy, politics).

Once a triggering event or focus event occurs, the three streams are joined to open a new opportunity window thereby a new creative decision making will occur. The examples are frequently found in the contemporary social and natural disasters, for instance, 911 Terrorism or COVID-19 Crisis.

1) **Problem Stream**: Problem consists of conflict, crisis, and a mix of these indicators. Until the triggering event, such as a dramatic event or political event, it flows independently by its logic and stream.

2) **Policy Stream**: Policy consists of the activities of policy entrepreneurs, and the pressure from interest groups. It also flows by its logic and stream.

3) **Politics Stream**: Politics consists of a change of government or parliamentary powers, social mood, and national atmosphere. It also flows by its logic and stream.

Figure 5-6	Policy Stream Model

Kingdon Model: Agendas, Alternatives, and Public Policies(1984)

Policy Stream

Policy Opportunity Window
Problem, Policy, and Political independently
flows and Coupled when the Triggering(Focus) event occurs

Stream of Problem	Stream of Politics	Stream of Policy
• Problem Consist of Conflict, Crisis, and a mix of these Indicators • Until Triggering Event, such as a Dramatic event or Political event, it flows independently by its own Logic and Stream	• Politics consists of Change of Government or Parliamentary Powers, social mood or national atmosphere • It also flows by its own Logic and Stream	• Policy consists of the activities of Policy Entrepreneurs • It also flows by its own Logic and Stream

Allison Model

Allison's model is suggested by G. Allison who wrote "Essence of Decision(1971)." As a famous scholar of public policy, he analyzed a Cuban Missile Crisis at which the former Secretary of the Soviet Union, Mr. Khrushchev, and President John F. Kennedy of the USA confronted each other with a high level of tension of collision around the Cuba Nuclear Missile Sites.

1) **Rational Actor.** The first model was the Rational Actor Model, or called the Allison Model I. It assumes the government is an organized and controlled organism having a unitary goal.

2) **Organizational Process**: The second model was the Organizational Process Model, or called Allison Model II. It assumes that the government has consisted of loosely coupled Sub-Organizations and therefore the goal of the nation sometimes conflicts with the goals of sub-organizations.

3) **Bureaucratic Politics**: The third model was the Bureaucratic Politics Model, or called Allison Model III. It assumes that the government has consisted of the even independent individual political actors surrounding the President. Therefore, the top decision-makers of the nation depend on the political resources of high-level individual actors centering on the President. The political goal of individual actors frequently conflicts with each other as we can see the words of hard-liners(Hawk) and soft-liners(Pigeon).

Figure 5-7	Allison Model

G. Allison, Essence of Decision(1971)

Division	Rational Actor	Organizational Process	Bureaucratic Politics
Organization	Organized and Controlled Organism	Association of loosely coupled Sub-Organizations	Aggregation of Independent Individual Political Actors
The Subject of Power	Top Leader of the Organization	Distributed to Semi-Independent Sub-Organizations	Depends on The Political Resources of High-level Individual Actors
Actor's Goal	The Unitary Goal	Goal of The Organization as A whole+Goals of Sub-Organizations	Goal of The Organization as A whole+Goals of Sub-Organizations +Goal of Individual Actors
Sharing Goals	Very strong	Weak	Very weak
Modality of Policy Decision	Top Leader: Command &Control Tower The Brain of Organization	SOP Program Repertoire	Conflict, Tensions, and Bargains Political Games
Consistency of Policy Decisions	Very strong (Always unitary &consistent)	Weak (Often changed)	Very weak (Almost not aligned)

▌ Agenda Setting Model

Definition

Agenda Setting is an act of the government adopting social problems as a government agenda. It means that once adopted it dictates the direction of the government decision. So, it is important as it is the first step of the policy process and thereby impacting on the next policy process. Hence, it is indispensable to search for a creative policy instrument at this stage using scientific foresight technology.

Figure 5-8	Agenda Setting Theory

Significance of Agenda Setting

Concept
• Agenda Setting is an act of the government adopting social problems as a government agenda.   • It means that once adopted it dectates the direction of government decision.

Importance
• The first step of the policy process: • Impact on the next policy process: • Hence, it is necessary to identify the creative policy instrument at this stage using scientific future foresight.

Steps

Agenda Setting has the following steps: 1) social problem, 2) social issue, 3) public agenda, and finally, 4) government agenda.

1) **Social Problem**: First, a social problem is a situation that many people in society are not satisfied with the problem. COVID-19 is a good example.

2) **Social Issue**: Social problem, if being debated by many people, it becomes a social issue. In the case of COVID-19, it immediately became a social

issue.

3) **Public Agenda**: When the social problem that is worthy of public attention, we call it a public agenda. Here the key factor is many people's critical interests, which was the vivid case of COVID-19.

4) **Government Agenda**: Finally, the public agenda will become a government agenda. As we can see in the case of COVID-19, this kind of immediate concern of the people will become the government and policy agenda quickly.

| Figure 5-9 | Policy Agenda Setting Theory |

Steps

Social Problem	• A situation that many people in society are not satisfied with the defects. * Example: COVID-19 Crisis
Social Issue	• Social problem, if being debated by many people, it becomes a social issue. * Key factor: Leadership or Triggering Event (dramatic event or political event)
Public Agenda	• When the social problem that are worthy of public attention, we call it public agenda. * Key factor: Many people's critical interests.
Government Agenda	• The public agenda will become policy agenda.

Agenda Setting Models

Agenda Setting has the following models: 1) mobilization model, 2) external initiative model, and 3) internal bureaucracy model.

1) **Mobilization Model**: First, the mobilization model frequently occurs in developing countries, whereby the strong President wants to transform his nation into a strong state. President set up a government agenda to solve the problems of his nation. The example was the Samaeul Movement of President Park Jung Hee in Korea which saved the nation from the absolute poverty level.

2) **External Initiative Model**: Second, the external initiative model takes the steps from the outsides. In this case, civil society raises the issue from a social problem, public agenda, and to the government agenda.

3) **Internal Bureaucracy Model**: Third, the internal bureaucracy model occurs when some group of internal bureaucrats at the high level attempts to proceed with some kind of policy with a secret movement. So, it is called a type of conspiracy model, which may not be desirable.

For the other types, there are policy stream model and advocacy coalition model, which we will discuss in the Policy Change Model section.

Figure 5-10 Agenda Setting Theory

Typology

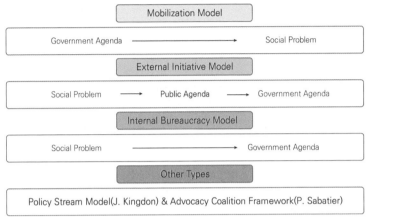

Policy Change Model

Definition

Policy Change is very important for policy innovation. After implementation, we need to monitor and evaluate what has happened and change to the new more creative initiatives.

Under the traditional Bureaucracy theory, we understood the policy change as termination.

But under the modern New Governance theory, we need to understand the fundamental characteristics of the policy process: dynamics, complexity, and circulation. The desirable policy change using foresight technologies is so critical for Effective & Creative policymaking. At this point, it may be useful to know Why the government can't do policy innovation or change? There are three reasons: 1) high cost, 2) political burden, 3) resistance to change.

Figure 5-11 **Obstacles**

Obstacle Factor: Why government cannot policy innovation or change?

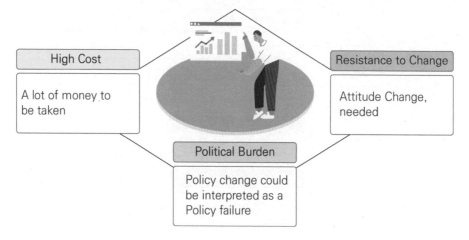

Also, we need to know there are four stages of policy change: 1) policy innovation, 2) policy maintenance, 3) policy succession, and 4) policy termination.

1) **Policy Innovation**: It means a new policy to intervene in the new area.

2) **Policy Maintenance**: It means maintaining the basic characteristics of the policy.

3) **Policy Succession**: It means a succession of the policy. There is simple succession and complex succession. Complex succession will change the basic nature of the existing policy(budget, staff, and organization).

4) **Policy Termination**: It means a termination of the policy. The business operation and budget will be extinguished at this stage.

Figure 5-12	Policy Change

Definition

Policy change and Future foresight

- Under the traditional Bureaucracy theory, we understood the policy change as termination.
- Under the modern New Governance theory, however, dynamics, complexity, and circulation.
- Policy Change for Effective & Creative Policy −Making will open the New Future & Innovation.

Four Types of Policy Change

Policy Innovation	Policy Maintenance	Policy Succession	Policy Termination
• Decide new policy to intervene the new area.	• Maintaining the basic characteristics.	• There are simple succession and complex succession. • Complex succession will change the basic nature of existing policies (budget, staff, and organization).	• The business operation and budget will be extinguished at this tage.

Basic Models

Let's examine the following diagram which shows the useful policy change model using the existing policy models: Policy Stream Model, Advocacy Coalition Model, and Policy Stage Model.

1) **Policy Stream**: First, it highlights the policy stream model which says that problem, policy, and politics flows independently before the triggering

event occurs. Once the triggering event happens, the policy window will open for a new paradigm of policy.

2) **Advocacy Coalition**: When the policy window opens, it is important to understand who supports the new policy and who opposes it. The belief and resource are two critical components gauging the strength of the group, advocacy group, and anti-advocacy group which basically will tell us who is going to be the winner of the policymaking.

3) **Policy Stage**: From agenda setting, policymaking, to policy implementation and evaluation, all going through the policy stage, it is very important to elucidate this fundamental dynamics of policy change which will lead to whether success or failure.

Figure 5-13 **Policy Change for Effective Policy Making**

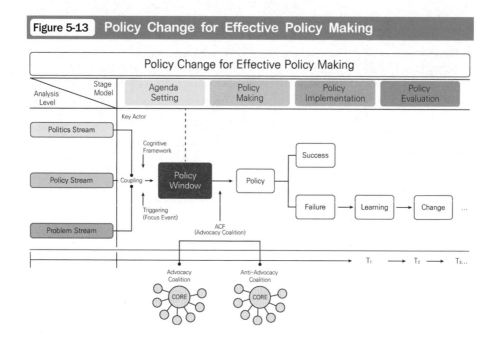

Hofferbert Model

Hofferbert's model dictates that there are five critical factors for policy change:

1) Historical & Geographical conditions

2) Socio-economic Conditions

3) Domestic Politics

4) Government Institution, and

5) Elite Behavior

These are direct and indirect factors affecting policy change like a spiral cubic way as shown below.

Figure 5-14	Policy Change Model

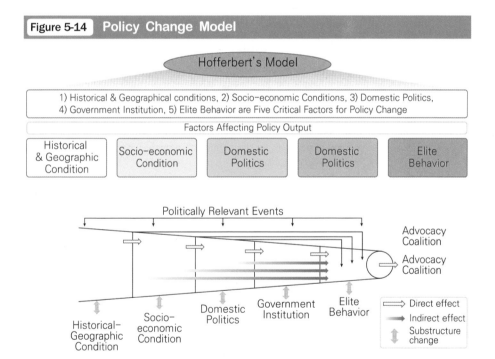

Sabatier Model

Sabatier's model dictates that two coalitions are affecting the policy: advocacy and anti-advocacy. The important factors are their belief and resources. Belief consists of belief core, policy core, and secondary aspects.

Also, in this ACF model, it is important to notice that there are two kinds of policy environment: stable and dynamic. The stables are the basic social structure, legal structure, and culture. And the dynamics are changes in economics such as oil prices or the regime change.

Figure 5-15 **Policy Change Model**

Sabatier's ACF Model

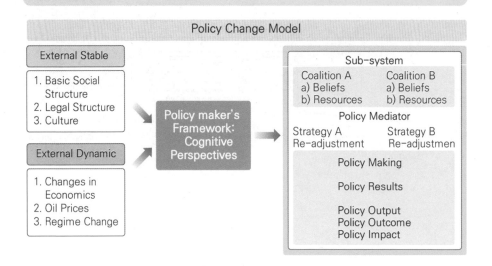

Macaroni Model

The Macaroni model dictates that there are two contexts affecting the policy: issue and institution. The issue context is like policy content or the level of appeal to the national opinion. The institutional context is more institutional factors relating to whether the President or ruling party supports which side. He argued that the institutional factor is more important than the issue factor as shown below. When the institutional context is favorable even if the issue context is not, the fortune maintains. On the other hand, if the institutional context is not favorable, regardless of issue context, the fortune collapses or decline at best.

Figure 5-16	Policy Change Model

Mucciaroni's IGF Model

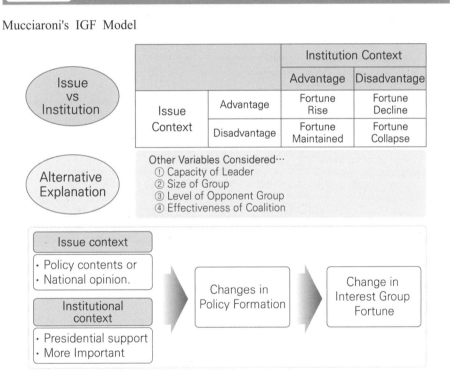

			Institution Context	
			Advantage	Disadvantage
Issue Context	Advantage		Fortune Rise	Fortune Decline
	Disadvantage		Fortune Maintained	Fortune Collapse

Other Variables Considered···
① Capacity of Leader
② Size of Group
③ Level of Opponent Group
④ Effectiveness of Coalition

Issue context
· Policy contents or
· National opinion.

Institutional context
· Presidential support
· More Important

Changes in Policy Formation

Change in Interest Group Fortune

Kingdon Model

The Kingdon model dictates that there are basically three streams affecting the policy: problem, policy, and politics. While they flow independently, the most important factor is the Triggering event, or Focus event, which consists of a dramatic event or political event. Good examples are the COVID-19 Crisis and the 911 Terrorism.

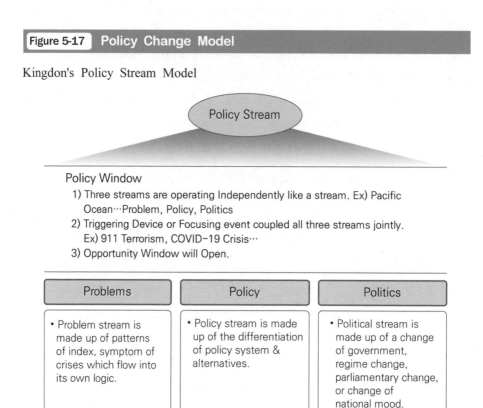

| Figure 5-17 | Policy Change Model |

Kingdon's Policy Stream Model

Policy Stream

Policy Window
1) Three streams are operating Independently like a stream. Ex) Pacific Ocean···Problem, Policy, Politics
2) Triggering Device or Focusing event coupled all three streams jointly. Ex) 911 Terrorism, COVID-19 Crisis···
3) Opportunity Window will Open.

Problems	Policy	Politics
• Problem stream is made up of patterns of index, symptom of crises which flow into its own logic.	• Policy stream is made up of the differentiation of policy system & alternatives.	• Political stream is made up of a change of government, regime change, parliamentary change, or change of national mood.

Hall Model

Hall's model dictates that policy change is like a paradigm change. When the normal times, Policymakers act within his framework of certain thoughts & beliefs, we call it attitude. But as anomalies increase, skepticism increases, the new paradigm is emerging as Tomas Kuhn aptly noted in his famous book, "The Structure of Scientific Revolution." As Quantum physics emerged, the previous Newton physics faded. Likewise, the Smart policy framework 4.0 with an effective policy making has emerged, the previous traditional bureaucratic model based on analog thinking fades away.

| Figure 5-18 | Policy Change Model |

Hall's Paradigm Change Model

| Concept | Fundamental policy changes are made possible by paradigm shifts |

| Policy Paradigm | Policy makers act in the framework of certain thoughts & beliefs⋯
But with an external shock, change the paradigm⋯
ex) Newton physics vs Quantum physics⋯
Traditional bureaucracy vs Smart policy framework 4.0 |

Policy Process Model

Definition

Policy Process starts with the basic question, who dominates the policy process: Elite or Plural group; Corporatism; Sub Government model, the Policy community, and Issue network. It is the topic regarding the Power Model perspective: Who Governs? Or Who dominates the policy process?

Before addressing this crucial issue, first, we need to understand the two faces of the policy process: one with a rational aspect, the other with the political aspect. The rational aspect consists of 1) rational policy instrument, 2) professionalism, and scientific process, while political aspect consists of 1) conflict of interests, 2) political game, and 3) political power.

Figure 5-19 Policy Process Model: Power Model

Two Faces of Policy Process

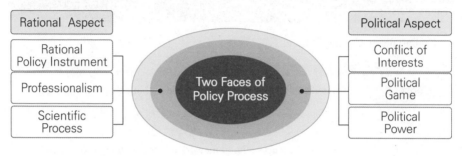

Elite Model

The Elite model says that the policy process is dominated by the Elite Group. There are three schools of thought in this elite theory.

1) **Classical Theory**: It is the theory of Mosca, Pareto, Michaels and it is the Philosophy of Iron Triangle. The theory argued that the ruling elite group is basically homogeneous and exclusive and not responsible for other classes. It is the unchanging truth regardless of any historical time in human life, they argued.

2) **The 1950's USA**: The elite theory in the 1950s in the United States showed two tracks: one with a position approach done by Mills and the other with a reputation approach done by Hunter. The Position approach analyzed the US power elites at the federal level, the government leader, army general, and global chairpersons, while the Reputation approach analyzed the 40 local experts at Atlanta. And they concluded that the policy process is dominated by the Elites.

3) **The New Elite Theory**: The new elite theory was argued by Bachrach and Baratz when they criticized the Pluralism of R. Dahl. Bachrach and Baratz criticized R. Dahl for not considering the aspects of the Non-decision Making Theory. This theory highlighted that there are two faces of public

policy: the bright side and the dark side. The dark side refers to the situation that the ruling elite group always suppresses the issues challenging directly or indirectly against their interests. Therefore, R. Dahl's conclusion of pluralism, presumably only considered the bright side, was misleading.

Figure 5-20   Policy Process Model: Elite Model

Elite Model

Three Schools of Elite Theory			
1. Classical Theory	2. 1950's U.S.A.		3. New Elite Theory
• Mosca, Pareto, Michaels: Philosophy of Iron Triangle • Clarified the Ruling Group and Subjugated Class • Homogeneous and Exclusive Elites • Not Responsible to Other Class • Regardless of Any Historical Time	• Mills • Position Approach (Analysis of policy process at the level of U.S. nationwide) * U.S. Power Elite: Government Leader-Army General- Global Chairperson	• Hunter • Reputation Approach (Analysis of policy process of Atlanta, U.S.) * Analyzed the most influential 40 local experts * Policy direction is decided and implemented by the Elites	• Bachrach • Baratz • Criticize the Pluralism of R. Dahl • Non-decision Making Theory : the decision which suppresses the issues challenging directly or potentially to the interests of ruling group by allowing the discussion only compatible with the ruling elite group

Pluralist Model

The Pluralist model says that the policy process is not dominated by a few Elites but by the diverse Plural Group. There are three schools of thought in this pluralist theory.

1) **Interest Group Theory**: It is the theory of Bentley & Truman who provided the early theoretical framework for pluralism. They argued that the articulation of various interest groups is beautiful for the principle of democracy as they reflect the needs of various interest groups and playing group dynamics under the principle of check and balance.

2) **Pluralism Theory**: It is the theory of R. Dahl who wrote a beautiful book, "Who Governs?" In this book, he analyzed as much as 170-year data in New Heaven city and concluded that Power is not just concentrated in a few dominant elite groups, but is widely distributed. And Interest groups have similar accessibility to those influences. Also, elite groups are circulating.

3) **New Pluralism Theory**: It is the Pluralism in modern times. Recognizing the special importance of the global Multinational corporate group & Government, they allow some exceptions to those two groups. Nevertheless, it also basically argued that the core power of the democratic society is more or less equally distributed and functioning well through the check & balance mechanism.

| Figure 5-21 | Policy Process Model: Pluralist Model |

Pluralism

Three Schools of Pluralism		
1. Interest Group theory	2. Puralism theory	3. New Pluralism theory
• Bentley & Truman Early theoretical framework of pluralism : They argued the articulation of many interest groups is beautiful as they Reflects the needs of various interest groups and Shows a Group Dynamics like check & balance.	• R. Dahl • Who Governs? : 1780-1950 Analysis of policy decision New Haven, USA for 170 years Power is not only concentrated in a few dominant elite groups, but is widely distributed. And Interest groups have the similar accessibility to those influence. Also, elite groups are Circulating.	• Criticism of Classical Pluralism * Recognizing that global Multi-national corporate group & Government is an exception. * Nevertheless, argued basically the core power of the democratic society is more or less equally distributed and functioning well through the check & balance mechanism.

Corporatism Model

Before studying the Sub-Government model, it is useful to examine the Corporatism model. Corporatism refers to the situation that the nation-state intentionally adjusts and controls the societal interests through coordinating social groups and individuals to induce society in a certain direction.

There are two types of Corporatism: National Corporatism and Social Corporatism.

1) **National Corporatism** is the situation where the Authoritarian state coordinates using top-organized social groups by the state authority. The example of Social Corporatism is the Italian Fascist Corporatism.

2) **Social Corporatism** is the situation that Corporatism is processed by an upward mechanism coordinated by the various social groups. The examples are the labor-management-political coalition case in the Netherlands (1982), Ireland Social Solidarity Convention (1987), and the Swedish Tripartite Convention (1988).

The positive functional aspects of Corporatism, assisted by digital capacities, national implementation of the delivery system would be effective at the maximum level. This was the case of the South Korean response system toward the COVID-19 crisis. Its delivery system, whether it was face-masks or national emergency disaster grants, was very effective by using the mediating agencies such as local drugstores and financial agencies.

Figure 5-22	Policy Process Model: Power Model

Corporatism

> ■ The nation state intentionally adjusts and controls the societal interests Through coordinating social groups and individuals to induce society toward a certain direction.

| 1. Speed: Speedy Problem Solving
2. Wisdom: 1. National Corporatism

   Authoritarian state coordinates
   using top-organized
   social groups by the state
   authority.

Example:
Italian Fascist Corporatism | 2. Social Corporatism

   This is processed by upward
   mechanism coordinated by the
   various social groups.

Examples: labor-management-political
group coalition
Netherlands (1982);
Ireland Social Solidarity Convention
(1987);
Swedish Tripartite Convention (1988) |

Sub-Government Model

The Sub-Government model says that the policy process is dominated by a tripartite coalition consisting of high-ranking government officials, standing chair of the parliament committee, and top CEO of a big national interest group. They make a Sub-Government system and usually set the basic stones of policy decisions nationwide. It is almost identical to the Iron Triangle concept. But the Sub-Government model has a more neutral meaning. It is a largely accepted model in the United States and Korea.

Figure 5-23 Policy Process Model: Sub-Governmental Model

Sub-Governmental Model

Policy process is dominated by a tripartite coalition consisted of high-ranking government officials, standing chair of the parliament committee, and top CEO of a big national interest group; Setting the basic stones of policy decisions nationwide.

High-ranking Government officials, standing chair of parliament committee, Top CEO of a big national interest group form a Sub-Governmental system

Top elites maintain a very close contact with each other

It is almost identical to the Iron Triangle concept; but the Sub-Government system has a more neutral meaning(US, Korea)

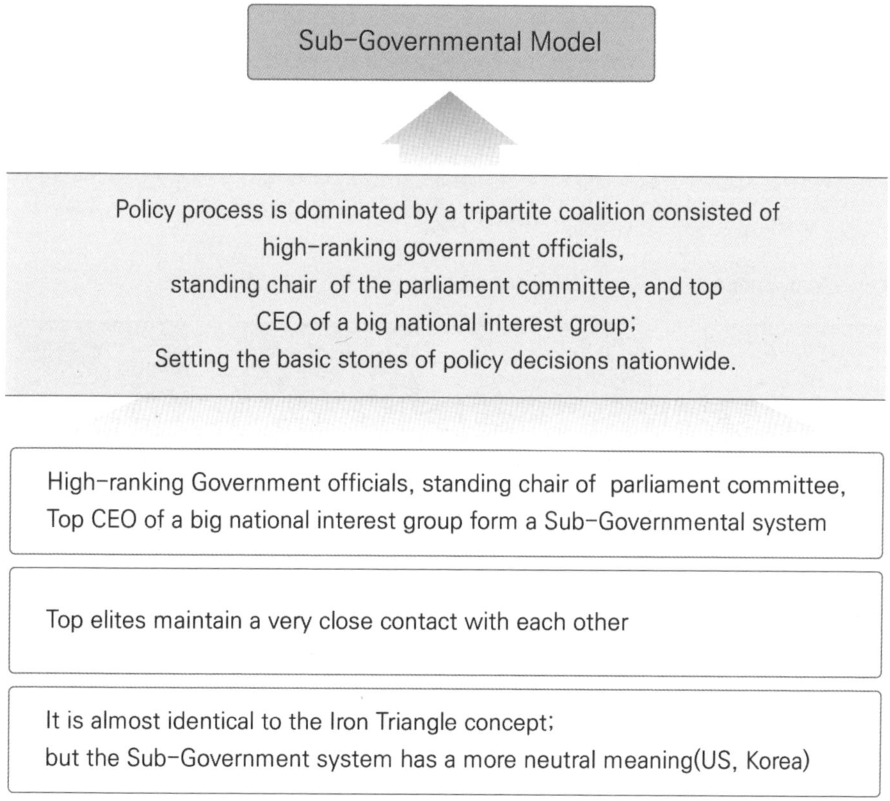

Policy Network Model

The Policy Network model is argued by Rhodes & Marsh who says that in the modern policy process it is very important to analyze policy networks among the key participants. When analyzing, it is important to notice the four critical components of policy network: 1) Policy Actors: who are the stakeholders, 2) Pattern: Configuration: whether they are harmonious or clustered separately, 3) Degree: Density: whether they closely cooperate or not, and 4) Policy Results: success or failure.

Figure 5-24 | Policy Process Model: Policy Network Model

Policy Network Model

> Concept:
> ■ Rhodes & Marsh proposed a policy network model that integrates the policy community model and the issue network model.

Key Components

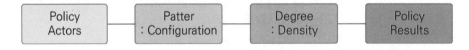

Finally, there are three distinct types of policy networks: Sub Government Model, Policy Community, and Issue Network. From Sub-Government Model to Policy Community and Issue Network, the pattern of interactions are from closed to more open. For example, the number of participants in the Sub-Government Model is very limited. But as closer to Policy Community and Issue Network the membership is more opened.

Figure 5-25 Policy Process Model: Policy Network Model

Sub-Government, Policy Community, and Issue Network

Type	Number of Participants	Key Actors	Inter-Dependence	Exclusive Membership	Relationship Persistence
Sub-Government Model	Limit	Government officials, National Assembly Standing Committee, Interest Group (Iron Triangle Alliance)	High	High	High
Policy Community	Extensive	Three Groups + Expert group	Relatively low	Relatively low	Relatively low
Issue Network	Very Extensive	Three Groups + Expert group + Other Journalists, Entrepreneurs etc.	Low (Looseness)	Low (Openness)	Low (Liquidity)

Summary and Conclusions: The Successful Conditions for Effective Policy Making

In this chapter, we elucidated the policy model approach for effective policymaking. As for the policy model, we highlighted the policy making model, agenda-setting model, policy change model, and policy process model.

First, for the policy making model, we reviewed the rational model, satisfying model, incremental model, mixed-scanning, optimal model, garbage can, policy stream, and Allison model among others.

Second, for the agenda-setting model, we reviewed the mobilization model, external initiative model, and internal bureaucracy model.

Third, for the policy change model, we reviewed the Hofferbert model, the Sabatier model, the Mucciaroni model, the Kingdon model, and the Hall model.

Finally, for the policy process model, we reviewed the Elite model, Pluralism model, Sub Government model, and Issue Network model.

Before closing this chapter, I would like to emphasize the conditions for successful and effective policymaking: People, Process, and Product. For the people aspect, we need to have an attitude change and capacity building for a better human resource and HRD. For the process aspect, we need to have an agile governance and cost reduction for better policy process management. As a result, we will have a great quality of the final product, which can be expressed as effective policy making and building a strong and great nation, as mentioned in chapter 1. In brief, we need a good direction with agility. Here, agility means a more speedy and flexible response.

Figure 5-26 **EFFECTIVE POLICY MAKING: CONDITIONS**

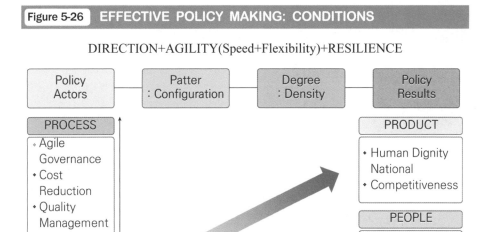

DIRECTION+AGILITY(Speed+Flexibility)+RESILIENCE

Policy Actors — Patter : Configuration — Degree : Density — Policy Results

PROCESS
- Agile Governance
- Cost Reduction
- Quality Management

PRODUCT
- Human Dignity National
- Competitiveness

PEOPLE
- Attitude Change, Capacity Building
- Strategic e-HRD, Certificate, e-Learning

Key Point!

1. Policy Making Model

Rational Model

▶ Rational Model is an economic model based on human reason & rationality. Neoclassic economists assumed the complete rationality such as 1) Complete Understanding of the Problem, 2) Precisely Define the Goal, 3) Identification of All Alternatives, 4) Sufficient Resources, and 5) Choosing the best Optimal Option.

Satisfying Model

▶ Satisfying Model is suggested by H. Simon who criticized the limitations of Rational Models. He suggested limited cognitive rationality, called a Bounded Rationality.

Incremental Model

▶ An incremental model is suggested by Lindblom &Widavsky who argued that making a gradual & partial change is better . It is the model based on organization and budget rationality.

Mixed Scanning Model

▶ Mixed Scanning model is suggested by A. Etzioni who argued that it is not ideal to just adopt one of the Rational Models or the Incremental Model.

Optimal Model

▶ The optimal model is suggested Y. Dror who criticized the Incremental Model. He also criticized the Rational Model saying that only economic efficiency is not enough. Rather he highlighted the Super-rationality by emphasizing the importance of systematic learning, originality, and creativity.

Garbage Can Model

▶ The Garbage Can model is suggested by J. March and J. Olsen who characterized the policy decision situation that is made in a very weak and confused state of cohesion.

Policy Stream Model

▶ The Policy Stream model is suggested by J. Kingdon who wrote "Agendas, Alternatives, and Public Policies(1984)." He suggested three streams independently flow: problem, policy, and politics.

1) Problem Stream: Problem consists of conflict, crisis, and a mix of these indicators. Until the triggering event, such as a dramatic event or political event, it flows independently by its logic and stream.
2) Policy Stream: Policy consists of the activities of policy entrepreneurs, and the pressure from interest groups. It also flows by its logic and stream.
3) Politics Stream: Politics consists of a change of government or parliamentary powers, social mood, and national atmosphere. It also flows by its logic and stream.

Allison Model

▶ Allison's model is suggested by G. Allison who wrote "Essence of Decision(1971)." As a famous scholar of public policy, he analyzed a Cuban Missile Crisis and suggested the following three models.

1) Rational Actor: The first model was the Rational Actor Model, or called the Allison Model I. It assumes the government is an organized and controlled organism having a unitary goal.

2) Organizational Process: The second model was the Organizational Process Model, or called Allison Model II. It assumes that the government consists of loosely coupled Sub-Organizations and therefore the goal of the nation sometimes conflicts with the goals of sub-organizations.

3) Bureaucratic Politics: The third model was the Bureaucratic Politics Model, or called Allison Model III. It assumes that the government consists of the even independent individual political actors surrounding the President.

2. Agenda Setting Model

1) Mobilization Model: First, the mobilization model frequently occurs in developing countries, whereby the strong President wants to transform his nation into a strong state. President set up a government agenda to solve the problems of his nation.

2) External Initiative Model: Second, the external initiative model takes the steps from the outsides. In this case, civil society raises the issue from a social problem, public agenda, and to the government agenda.

3) Internal Bureaucracy Model: Third, the internal bureaucracy model occurs when some group of internal bureaucrats at the high level attempts to proceed with some kind of policy with a secret movement. So, it is called a type of conspiracy model, which may not be desirable.

3. Policy Change Model

Sabatier Model

▶ Sabatier's model says that there are basically two coalitions affecting the policy: advocacy and anti-advocacy. The important factors are their belief and resources. Belief consists of belief core, policy core, and secondary aspects.

Macaroni Model

▶ **The Macaroni** model says that there are basically two contexts affecting the policy: issue and institution. The issue context is like policy content or the level of appeal to the national opinion. The institutional context is more institutional factors relating to whether the President or ruling party supports which side.

Kingdon Model

▶ **The Kingdon** model says that there are basically three streams affecting the policy: problem, policy, and politics. While they flow independently, the most important factor is the Triggering event, or Focus event, which consists of a dramatic event or political event. Good examples are the COVID-19 Crisis and the 911 Terrorism.

Hall Model

▶ Hall's model says that policy change is like a paradigm change. When the normal times, Policymakers act within his framework of certain thoughts & beliefs, we call it attitude. But as anomalies increase, skepticism increases, then the new paradigm is emerging as Tomas Kuhn aptly noted in his famous book, "The Structure of Scientific Revolution."

▶ For example, the Smart policy framework 4.0 with effective policy making has emerged, the previous traditional bureaucratic model based on analog thinking fades away.

4. Policy Process Model

Elite Model

▶ **The Elite** model says that the policy process is dominated by the Elite Group. There are three schools of thought in this elite theory.

1) Classical Theory: It is the theory of Mosca, Pareto, Michaels and it is

the Philosophy of Iron Triangle.

2) The 1950's USA: The elite theory in the 1950s in the United States showed two tracks: one with a position approach done by Mills and the other with a reputation approach done by Hunter.

3) The New Elite Theory: The new elite theory was argued by Bachrach and Baratz. This theory highlighted the decision which suppresses the issues challenging directly or indirectly to the interests of the ruling elite group.

Pluralist Model

▶ The Pluralist model says that the policy process is not dominated by a few Elites but by the diverse Plural Group. There are three schools of thought in this pluralist theory.

1) Interest Group Theory: It is the theory of Bentley & Truman who provided the early theoretical framework for pluralism.

2) Pluralism Theory: It is the theory of R. Dahl who wrote a beautiful book, "Who Governs?" In this book, he analyzed as much as 170-year data in New Heaven city and concluded that Power is not just concentrated in a few dominant elite groups, but is widely distributed.

3) New Pluralism Theory: It is the Pluralism in modern times. Recognizing the special importance of the global Multinational corporate group & Government, they allow some exceptions to those two groups.

Corporatism Model

▶ There are two types of Corporatism: National Corporatism and Social Corporatism.

1) National Corporatism is the situation where the Authoritarian state coordinates using top-organized social groups by the state authority. The example of Social Corporatism is the Italian Fascist Corporatism.

2) Social Corporatism is the situation that Corporatism is processed by an

upward mechanism coordinated by the various social groups. The examples are the labor-management-political coalition case in the Netherlands (1982), Ireland Social Solidarity Convention (1987), and the Swedish Tripartite Convention (1988).

Sub-Government Model

▶ **The Sub-Government** model says that the policy process is dominated by a tripartite coalition consisting of high-ranking government officials, standing chair of the parliament committee, and top CEO of a big national interest group. They make a Sub-Government system and usually set the basic stones of policy decisions nationwide.

Policy Network Model

▶ **The Policy** Network model is argued by Rhodes & Marsh who says that in the modern policy process it is very important to analyze policy networks among the key participants.

▶ There are three distinct types of policy networks: Sub Government Model, Policy Community, and Issue Network. From Sub-Government Model to Policy Community and Issue Network, the pattern of interactions are from closed to more open.

| Figure 5-27 | Discussion Question: Policy Model |

| Effective Policy Making | • What are the important Policy Making Models?
• What is the Allison I, II, III Model? How does it associated with Cuban Missile Crisis?
• What is the Kingdon's PS Model? Explain with the Case of the COVID-19 Crisis.
• What is the Sabatier's ACF Model?
• Explain with the Case of Pro and Anti-Nuclear Power Plant Energy Policy.
• What would be the most appropriate model explaining your policy issues at hand?
• Select one best model and Explain how does it apply to explain your policy issue? |

| Figure 5-28 | Team Assignment for Design Stage |

| Effective Policy Making | * Team Assignment for Design Stage:
• For Each team, Please presents the effective policy design by addressing the current obstacles in your area and the desirable strategic solutions to overcome those obstacles:
• For example, if you are the member of the H.E.I(Health, Employment, Industry4.0) Ministry Team, consider these issues: What are the problems? How to handle the employment issues, such as the unemployment risks faced by the Industry 4.0. How to restructuring industrial structures by utilizing Smart technologies and Smart e-government.
• If you are the Vision Team, especially focus on the strategic solutions using Smart government, industrial structures, and digital technologies. |

PART 3

POLICY ANALYSIS & IMPLEMENTATION

Chapter 6

POLICY ANALYSIS & EVALUATION
The Methodology Approach for Effective Policy Making

> Policy analysis and evaluation is the key to the policy capacity building by providing fundamental methodologies and skills for effective policymaking.

≫ Objectives

The purpose of this chapter is to elucidate the theory and methodologies of policy analysis and policy evaluation. To ensure effective policy making, we need to learn the skills and methodologies to analyze the complex dimensions of public policy. This chapter will highlight the foresight skills which are the most updated technologies of policy analysis.

First, for policy analysis, it will highlight the important theories and methodological skills of the quantitative approach as well as the qualitative approach. For the quantitative approach, it will review theoretical modeling, regression analysis, and simulation with sensitivity analysis. For the qualitative approach, it will review the Classic Delphi, Policy Delphi, Cross Impact Analysis, and Feasibility Analysis. And this chapter will also review the critical issues of Policy Design, Policy Criteria, and Comprehensive Policy Design Table and its Analytic components for effective policy analysis.

Second, for policy evaluation, it will highlight the important theories and methodological skills of experiment and non-experiment(called

Statistics). It will address the issues including 1) What are the true conditions for a true experiment? 2) What are causal inference and its conditions? 3) What are validity and reliability? And finally, 4) What is the desirable process for effective policy evaluation?

The Methodology Approach to Effective Policy Making: Policy Analysis and Scientific Inquiry

To perform effective policy making it is critical to comprehend the fundamental methodologies of policy analysis. In other words, policy analysis is the key to the policy capacity building. If we cannot possess the working knowledge to perform the technical methodologies, we could not analyze the detailed policy problems and alternatives. Therefore, the public officials in developing countries must gain practical knowledge to exercise statistical analysis.

Scientific inquiry is very important. The public officials should always carry out a scientific inquiry such as: Why does this problem keep happening? What are the fundamental causes and reasons to affect this result? And what are the causal mechanisms between the independent variables and the dependent variable?

In fact, human curiosity and passion were a driving force leading to the scientific findings which enormously contributed to contemporary civilization. For instance, C. Darwin started with his simple inquiry, why some birds have different colors and shapes even though they are the same species. S. Freud started with his inquiry, what are the mechanisms of human being's sub and unconsciousness world. What could the analysis of the Libido and original desires contribute to solve our inherent problems inside the unconscious world? Finally, H. Lasswell also started with his inquiry, what kind of academic paradigm could solve the fundamental problems in our society so that people could realize their human dignity?

As mentioned earlier, in our society problem streams. When it becomes severe like COVID-19, it immediately becomes a policy agenda. Then, we should have an academic puzzle, for example, what would be the most effective policy framework to cope with the COVID-19 Crisis? If governments have experienced SARS and MERS before, why do some governments keep failing to quickly and effectively respond to the virus problem? And from comparative standpoints, what kind of policy framework would be more effective to protect the people within the nation?

A good analysis takes the following steps(see the following diagram below):
1) Having Academic Puzzles by asking what are the most fundamental problems in your society?
2) Setting up Hypotheses.
3) What is the Causal Relationship between the variables?
4) What is your Theoretical Argument?
5) What is our Empirical Model?
6) Perform Analysis using quantitative and qualitative methodologies: we will focus on these skills especially in this chapter. And finally
7) Findings: what are the policy implications, and what would be your most feasible recommendations?

From another angle, the good report takes the following steps:
1) Issues: Problem Definition
2) Best Practice: Benchmarking
3) Empirical Analysis
4) Evaluation for Policy Alternatives
5) Final Conclusion: It should include the expected problems like the financial resources and HRD issue.

And what should be the strategies to overcome those practical problems?

The best criteria assessing the policy alternatives are two-fold: desirability and feasibility. Desirability has six components: effectiveness, efficiency, equity, responsiveness, adequacy, and appropriateness. And feasibility has also six components: political, financial, social, administrative, legal, and technical feasibility.

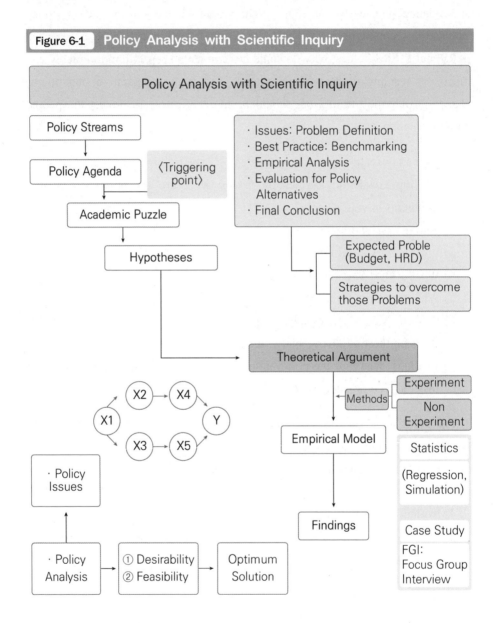

Figure 6-1 Policy Analysis with Scientific Inquiry

Analytical Tools(1): The Foresight Methodology as a Policy Analysis

Definition

Foresight is a tool to see the future. It is different from simple forecasting in the sense that forecasting is only quantitative data-based extrapolation in the future. Foresight, on the other hand, using both quantitative and qualitative methodologies, helps the top decision-maker to anticipate the expected scenario of a specific policy. Therefore, it is a very important technology to perform effective policy making. It has the following three functional values: 1) Providing Information: Providing policymakers with good information, 2) Controlling Policy: Successful control is possible, and 3) Future Value: Foresight will give you future value.

| Figure 6-2 | Future Foresight |

Definition: Functional Value

> ① Providing Information: Providing policy makers with good information.
> ② Controlling Policy : Successful control is possible
> ③ Future Value : Foresight will give you future value.

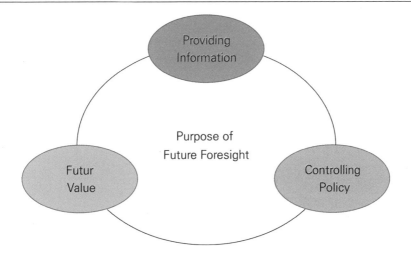

Quantitative Methodology

This is the most effective way to analyze. Three approaches stand out: 1) Theoretical Model, 2) Regression Analysis, 3) Simulation: Sensitivity Analysis.

1) **Theoretical Modelling**: Theoretical modeling means to confirm the causal relationship that would affect the policy outcomes by deducing the factors from the previous theories and articles and to clarify the causal relationship between policy measures(independent) and policy outcomes(dependent).

2) **Regression Analysis**: Regression analysis is the statistical method to estimate the direction and size of the relationship between the independent and dependent variables. It has two versions: 1) Cross-sectional analysis: Analysis unit is not time but analysis of the cross-sectional units, 2) Time-Series analysis: Analysis unit is time and longitudinal.

3) **Simulation**: Simulation or Sensitivity analysis is also very useful to give valuable information to the top decision-maker. By changing the value of the assumptions underlying the uncertainty, it is very helpful for decision making. The examples include the sensitivity analysis of public amusement parks whether to invest in it or not.

| Figure 6-3 | Quantitative Methodology(1) |

> ■ This is the most effective way to analyze. It is a Scientific Approach. Three
> approaches stand out: Theoretical Model, Regression Analysis, Simulation:
> Sensitivity Analysis.

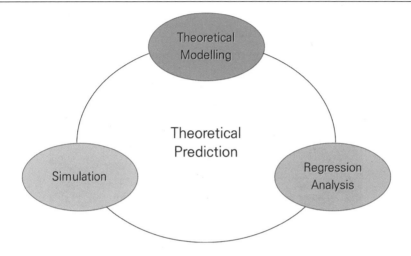

Qualitative Methodology

Qualitative methodology is also very important as in many cases public policy
cannot always express in quantified numbers.

1. Brainstorming:

These qualitative methods may start with Brainstorming. A good example was
the Cuban Missile Crisis Strategic Solution with Brainstorming. The US President
at the time, John F. Kennedy, after convening the Excom(National Security
Top-level Meeting), seriously talked to his top staff, "Tell me whatever it may
seem a silly & stupid idea"(John F. Kennedy).

He made a genuinely Free Atmosphere in which the free and creative idea
could be flowing out: no leader dictates the direction or intervention of the
discussion.

The flowing chart of the decision making at the time was like this: The first
dominating idea of Surgical Strike → Future Possibilities with Surgical

Strike(Futures Wheel) → What would then be the other Alternatives to Preventing the 3rd Nuclear World War(Decision Tree) → Naval Blockade(Final Policy Making).

Figure 6-4	Brainstorming

Case: Cuban Missile Crisis & Brainstorming

- Cuban Missile Crisis Strategic Solution with Brainstorming
- "Tell me whatever it may seem a silly & stupid idea"(John F. Kennedy)
- Excom(National Security Meeting): Brainstorming with National Top-Security Level Bureaucrats & Army Generals
- Discussion without Leader, Authoritarian Ruler → Genuinely Free Atmosphere
- Surgical Strike —►uture Possibilities with Surgical Strike(Futures Wheel) → hat would then be the other Alternative to Preventing the 3rd Nuclear World War(Decision Tree) —►aval Blockade(Final Policy Making).

2. Scenario Planning:

After Brainstorming you may proceed to Scenario Planning. For example, to predict what will be the future scenario for the smart cities: two positive scenarios of the favorable and ecological pattern: 1) horizontal extension of the city, 2) respond actively to climate change; and the other two negative scenarios of declining: 3) declining collapse of the city, and 4) respond passive to climate change, that is 1) prosperity with coexistence, 2) existing problems of machinery city, 3) dividing cities, and 4) declining and doomed collapse. The following figure illustrates the four future scenarios of smart cities sketching with the qualitative methodology of scenario planning.

Figure 6-5 Scenario Planning: The Future of Smart City

Optimum Solution

Optimum Solution

Optimum Solution

Optimum Solution

3. Classic Delphi

The Classic Delphi for foresight takes the following 4 steps:

1) **Round Questionnaire**: In this first step, the experts are required to propose technical tasks to predict the trends of a certain field, the topic of policy analysis, and complete the questionnaire. The research team summarizes the mean, median, and summary statistics of the 1st result and gives feedback to the original experts who gave the results in the first place.

Opportunities to revise forecasts based on the summary statistics.

2) **Round Questionnaire**: In this second step, the experts are given the opportunities to revise his forecasts based on the summary statistics. The research team repeats the above process.

3) **Round Questionnaire:** In this third step, the experts are given the opportunities to revise his forecasts based on the summary statistics. The research team repeats the above process.

4) **4 Round Questionnaire**: In this final step, the experts are given the opportunities to revise his forecasts based on the summary statistics. The research team repeats the above process and then finishes the Delphi process and finalizes the Results.

Figure 6-6	Qualitative Methodology(1): Classic Delphi for Foresight

CLASSIC DELPHI	1 Round Questionnaire	• Experts are required to propose technical tasks to be predicted the trends in a certain field, the topic to be analyzed. • Completed questionnaire. The research team summarizes the mean, median, and summary statistics of the 1st result to give feed back to the original experts.
	2 Round Questionnaire	• Opportunities to revise forecasts based on the summary statistics • Repeat above process
	3 Round Questionnaire	• Opportunities to revise forecasts based on the summary statistics • Repeat above process
	4 Round Questionnaire	• Opportunities to revise forecasts based on the summary statistics • Repeat above process • Finish the Process and finalize the Results

4. Policy Delphi

Definition: Policy Delphi is a revised and advanced version of the Classic Delphi and to develop the desirable policy alternatives by synthesizing the expert opinions on governmental policy issues.

Features: Policy Delphi has three features: 1) selective anonymity, 2) polarized statistical processing, and 3) intentionally framed the structured conflicts. The steps for Policy Delphi are as follows:

1. **Select carefully Delphi participants & designs questionnaire**
2. **Analyze the results of the responses**
3. **Repeat the process**
4. **Ignite the structured conflicts**
5. **Finalize report of findings**

Figure 6-7 **Qualitative Methodology(2): Policy Delphi for Foresight**

POLICY
Definition: The Delphi method is applied for the development of desirable alternatives by synthesizing the expert opinions on the governmental policy issues
Features: Selective anonymity, polarized statistical processing, intentionally framed the structured conflicts

DELPHI
① Select carefully Delphi participants & designs questionnaire
② Analyze the results of the responses
③ Repeat the process
④ Ignite the structured conflicts
⑤ Finalize Report of findings

5. Cross Impact Analysis

Definition: Cross Impact Analysis is the analytical tool to find the probability that one event will occur, and to calculate the probability that the remaining event will occur if the first event is preceded.

Features: The Cross Impact Analysis is an excellent methodology to show the following features of the forecasting event:

1. **Direction**
2. **Strength**
3. **Time Difference**

| Figure 6-8 | Qualitative Methodology(3): Cross Impact Analysis for Foresight |

Cross Impact Analysis

> ■ To find the probability that one event will occur, and to calculate the probability that the remaining event will occur if the first event is preceded.

6. Feasibility Analysis

Definition: Feasibility Analysis helps the Top-decision maker to forecast the expected result such as whether the policy bill will be passed or not. The Feasibility factors are as follows:

※ **Feasibility Factors:**
① **Key Actors**

② **Direction: Plus or Minus**
③ **Available Resources**
④ **Relative Impact**

Let's take an example. Let's assume that there are two alternatives available for a certain mayor:

1) to increase the income tax by 1 % average for a certain project
2) to make the fund by cutting the city budget.

In this case, the key actors are

1) mayor
2) city council such as the local parliamentary members
3) taxpayers
4) local government bureaucrats, and
5) leading press groups in the city

Available resources will be measured from 0 to 1 according to the factors of budget, staff, credibility, and informational resources. This measurement can be assessed by asking the experts using the Policy Delph mentioned above. Also, the relative impact can be assessed using the Policy Delph method.

Figure 6-9	Qualitative Methodology(4): Feasibility Analysis for Foresight

Feasibility Analysis

- Helps Top-decision maker to anticipate the expected result whether the policy bill will be passed or not

※ Feasibility Factors:
① Key Actors
② Direction: Plus or Minus
③ Available Resources
④ Relative Impact

Figure 6-10	Feasibility Analysis

* Policy A: 1 % Increase of Local Income Tax

Actors	Direction	Probability	Available Resources	Relative Impact	Feasibility Score
Mayor	+1	0.2	0.2	0.4	0.016
City Council	-1	0.6	0.7	0.8	-0.336
Tax Payers	-1	0.9	0.8	1.0	-0.720
Local Bureaucrats	+1	0.9	0.6	0.6	0.324
Press Group	+1	0.1	0.5	0.2	0.010

* Policy B: Cutting Budget

Actors	Direction	Probability	Available Resources	Relative Impact	Feasibility Score
Mayor	+1	0.8	0.2	0.4	0.192
City Council	+1	0.4	0.5	0.8	0.160
Tax Payers	+1	0.9	0.7	1.0	0.630
Local Bureaucrats	-1	0.9	0.8	0.6	-0.432
Press Group	-1	0.1	0.5	0.2	-0.010

Policy Design

Definition: Policy Design is to link Policy Instruments mutually to identify the Causal Relationships among the factors. Finding the causal mechanism is the key to Policy Analysis.

Critical Factors: The factors affecting the policy design are as follows:
1) the urgency of policy issues
2) strength of the related group
3) political situation
4) interests of stakeholders
5) policy goal, and
6) causal relationship

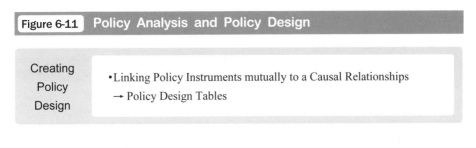

Figure 6-11   Policy Analysis and Policy Design

Creating Policy Design	• Linking Policy Instruments mutually to a Causal Relationships → Policy Design Tables

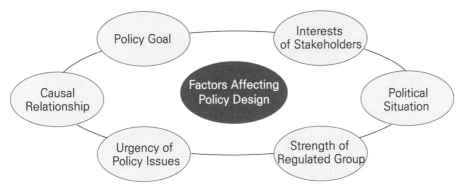

Policy Criteria

Definition: Policy Criteria is an important standard to evaluate policy alternatives. Analysis means "Look at it separately and compare." Therefore, Policy Analysis means "Analyze the policy into its Value according to its dimensions."

Dimension: The critical dimensions are four:

1) Productivity
2) Feasibility
3) Democracy, and
4) Reflexivity

Productivity means effectiveness and efficiency. Feasibility means political, economic, social, administrative, legal, and technical feasibility. Democracy means participation, deliberation, and consensus. Finally but not lastly, reflexivity means human dignity in which self-realization at the individual level and trustful and mature society at the community level.

Figure 6-12 Policy Analysis

New Criteria for Policy Analysis(1)

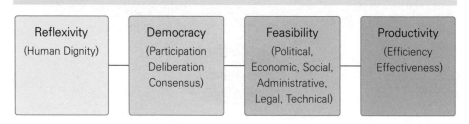

- Analysis: It means 'to look at it separately'.
- Policy Analysis means 'Analyze the policy into its value dimensions'.

| Reflexivity (Human Dignity) | Democracy (Participation Deliberation Consensus) | Feasibility (Political, Economic, Social, Administrative, Legal, Technical) | Productivity (Efficiency Effectiveness) |

Logical Grounds: It is important to set up the policy criteria to solve the problem through the governance approach in modern times. In this respect, the policy analysis criteria should be classified into three dimensions: productivity, democracy, and reflexivity. As shown in the below diagram, W. Dunn, the famous scholar of policy analysis, suggested the important criteria of desirability and feasibility but omitted the important dimension of democracy. As a result, the author presents the total comprehensive policy design table, by correcting the mentioned limitation of W. Dunn, as follows.

Figure 6-13 Policy Analysis

New Criteria for Policy Analysis(2)

It is important to set up the policy criteria to solve the problem through the governance approach in modern times. In this respect, the policy analysis criteria should be classified into the three dimensions: productivity, democracy, and reflexivity.

Scholar	Criteria	Detailed Criteria (W. Dunn)	Modified I (GH KWON)	Contents		Modified II (GH KWON)	Contents	
W.Dunn	Desirability	Adequacy Appropriateness Equity Responsiveness Effectiveness Efficiency	Substantive Desirability (Contents)	Adequacy Appropriateness Equity Responsiveness		Reflexivity	Human right, Justice Trust building Integrity	Substantive Value
				Effectiveness Efficiency		Productivity	Effectiveness Efficiency	Efficiency
		-	Procedural Desirability (Process)	Democracy	Participation Deliberation Agreement	Democracy	Democracy Transparency	Procedural Value
	Feasibility	Political Economical Social Administrative Legal Technical	Political Economical Social Administrative Legal Technical	Political Economical Social Administrative Legal Technical		Political Economical Social Administrative Legal Technical	Political Economical Social Administrative Legal Technical	Political Economical Social Administrative Legal Technical

Policy Design Table

Definition: It is necessary to set up the Policy Design Table to analyze the priorities among the policy alternatives. The total and comprehensive policy design table is as follows:

| Figure 6-14 | Policy Analysis |

Policy Design Table

It is necessary to set up the following Policy Design Table to analyze the priorities among policy alternatives.

Evaluation Dimension	Evaluation Contents Evaluation Items(Standard)		Alternatives Measures	Altern- ative 1	Altern- ative 2	Alterna- tive 3	...
Reflexivity	Dem- ocracy	Reflexivity	① Human Rights, Justice, Dignity				
			② Contribution to Trustful & Matured Community				
		Procedural Democracy	① Procedural Legality				
			② Procedural Validity				
		Substantive Democracy	① Degree of Participation				
			② Degree of Deliberation				
			③ Degree of Agreement				
Feasibility			① Political Feasibility				
			② Financial Feasibility				
			③ Social Feasibility				
			④ Administrative Feasibility				
			⑤ Legal Feasibility				
			⑥ Technical Feasibility				
Productivity			① Effectiveness				
			② Efficiency				
Overall Evaluation							

Analytical Elements

Reflexivity: It is policy criteria for the highest value of humanity. It is the realization of human dignity at the individual level and the realization of a trustful and mature society at the community level. The specific measuring index is

1) Appropriateness

2) Adequacy

3) Equity, and

4) Responsiveness.

Figure 6-15	Analytical Elemen

Dimensions and Index

Reflexivity	
Concept	Policy criteria for the Highest Value of Humanity
Component	Realization of Human Dignity (at individual level) Realization of Trustful and Matured Society (at community level)
Index	Appropriateness, Adequacy, Equity, Responsiveness

Democracy	
Concept	From bureaucracy to Governance society → Need Deliberative Democracy
Component	Procedural Democracy (Legality, Validity) Substantive Democracy (Degree of Participation, Deliberation, Consensus)

Democracy: It becomes more critical as society changes from bureaucracy to New Governance. Accordingly, we need a Deliberative Democracy more than ever before. This criterion has two critical elements:

1) Procedural Democracy (Legality, Validity), and

2) Substantive Democracy (Degree of Participation, Deliberation, Consensus)

Productivity: It is policy criteria to select the most effective and efficient policy option. The components are

1) Efficiency, and

2) Effectiveness

The methods to analyze these criteria are

1) Cost-Benefit Analysis, and

2) Cost-Effectiveness Analysis

The most popular methodology to compare the benefit and the cost, called PV(Present Value) and NPV(Net Present Value) is as follows. It is important because usually, the government project takes a long time so that you should not fail to calculate the net present value of the project. The following formula ensures the net present value as it takes into account the discount rate.

$$\text{Present Value (PV)} = \frac{F}{(1+r)^t}$$

F: Financial Value at future time t, r: discount rate from the industrial bank

$$\text{Net Present Value (NPV)} = \sum_{t=0}^{t=T} \frac{B_t}{(1+r)^t} - \sum_{t=0}^{t=T} \frac{C_t}{(1+r)^t}$$

Feasibility: It is policy criteria to assess the real feasibility of a certain policy alternative. It has two conceptual components:

1) Adoptability: The possibility of being adopted as a policy, and

2) Implementability

The possibility of being implemented as a policy. It also has six empirical components:

1) Political feasibility

2) financial feasibility

3) social feasibility

4) Administrative feasibility

5) legal feasibility, and

6) technical feasibility

The total feasibility index can be calculated as follows:

Total Feasibility Index=Direction*Available Resources*Relative Impact

Figure 6-16	Analytical Elements(2)

Dimensions and Index

Productivity	
Concept	Select the most Effective & Efficient Policy Option
Component	Effectiveness, Efficiency
Index	Cost–Benefit Analysis, Cost–Effectiveness Analysis

Feasibility	
Concept	The possibility of being adopted as a policy(Adoptability) The possibility of being implemented as a policy (Implementabilty)
Component	Political feasibility, financial feasibility, social feasibility, Administrative feasibility, legal feasibility, technical feasibility
Index	Total Feasibility Index=Direction*Available Resources *Relative Impact

Analytical Tools(2): Policy Evaluation

Definition

Policy Evaluation is another analytical tool for monitoring in the middle of implementation and final evaluation for the government's transparency and accountability.

Features

Policy Evaluation has the following three features:

1) **Focus:** It focuses on the Performance: output, outcome & impact.

2) **Criteria:** Efficiency, Effectiveness, Equity, Responsiveness, Adequacy (timing, degree), Appropriateness(value, trend, the spirit of the time: time, speed, uncertainty, VUCA).

3) **Careful Assessment:** It will find out whether it is necessary for government intervention, if any, then what kinds of intervention it needed?

| Figure 6-17 | Policy Evaluation |

Definition & Features

Definition	Policy Evaluation ⇒ Government needs to do Monitoring in the Middle & Final Evaluation for its Transparency and Accountability
Features	① Focus: It focuses on: Output, Outcome & Impact ② Criteria: Efficiency, Effectiveness, Equity, Responsiveness, Adequacy(timing, degree), Appropriateness(Value, Trend, Spirit of Time: time, speed, uncertainty, VUCA) ③ Careful Assessment: And Find out Whether Necessary for Government Intervention, if any, then What Kinds of Intervention?

Method and Experiment

Policy Evaluation needs to have a scientific method. It has two methods: experiment and non-experiment. The true experiment needs two conditions:

1) Random Assignment: Experiment group and Control group based on the randomization principle; otherwise, we would have a selection bias.

2) Treatment: And check the before and after Treatment.

We call it the policy or program effect. That the logic and rationale of the Experiment.

Figure 6-18   Policy Evaluation: Method and Experiment

Method

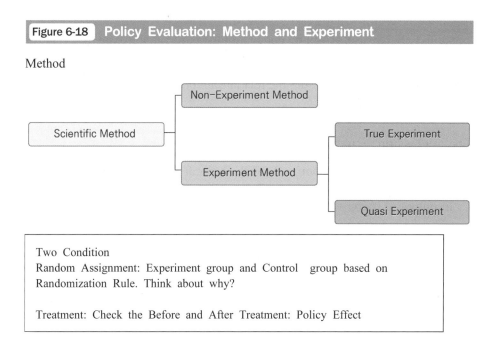

Two Condition
Random Assignment: Experiment group and Control group based on Randomization Rule. Think about why?

Treatment: Check the Before and After Treatment: Policy Effect

Causal Inference

Definition: Policy is an independent variable; policy outcome as a dependent variable. But we should ask, "Is that real? Does it actually happen?" to find out there exists a real Causal Relationship between the two variables.

Three Conditions: The three conditions for casual relationship are:

1) **Time Precedence:** The independent variable should occur before the dependent variable.

2) **Covariance:** There should exist correlation and covariance between the independent and dependent variable.

3) **Control Third Variable:** You should control the other background characteristics not to have a spurious or confounding effect.

Spurious and Confounding Effects: If you do not control the third variable, you may conclude the causal relationship even though it does not exist. We call it a Spurious effect. Also, If you do not control the third variable, you may find the effect with exaggeration or downward. We call it a Confounding effect. For example, if you want to measure the relationship between income and education among the young population.

The regression equation is like this:

Income$i$ = α + β_1(Education) + β_2(SES: Father or Mother's Wealth) + εi

In this case, if you fail to include the variable of SES, the estimation of the coefficient, b1 will be exaggerated in a positive way, which should be avoided. You may also think of including the gender, age, job experience and etc. to control and find out the real effect of education affecting the level of income.

Figure 6-19	Policy Evaluation

Causal Inference

Definition	■ Policy is an Independent variable; Policy Outcome as a Dependent variable; Is that Real? Actually Happened? Find out There Exists a real Causal Relationship between the Two variables.
Three Conditions	① Time Precedence: The Independent variable should occur before. ② Covariance : Correlation & Covariance between the Two variables. ③ Control Third Variable : Control the Other Background Characteristics.
Spurious & Confounding	① Spurious Effect: If you do not control the third variable, you may create a causal relationship even if it does not exist. ② Confounding Effect: If you do not control the third variable, you may exaggerate or reduce the relationship. ex) $\text{Income}_i = \alpha + \beta_1(\text{Education}) + \beta_2(\text{SES: Father or Mother's Wealth}) + \varepsilon_i$

Validity & Reliability

Validity: To ensure the real causal relationship, you need to understand the concept of validity and reliability. Validity is asking that your finding is really ensuring the real cause. It has two versions: internal validity and external validity. Internal validity is more critical as it is related to the issue of whether the effect is really due to the policy intervention or the other factors. Therefore, it is really important to have a research design in the right way by checking whether you included all the relevant factors in your equation and the relationship is really based on the sound and valid theory. External validity is about the generalization issue, meaning that whether your research findings can be applied in other circumstances, whether it is time or places.

Reliability: Reliability refers to the situation whether your research or evaluation is really reliable. If it does, we call it reliability or reproducibility. In other words, when the other person applies the same methodology and the same data, it should produce some empirical results. This the logic behind the scientific development in human history. The factors that reduce reliability are as follows:

1) Measurement Issue: Data or Questionnaire
2) Sensitive Reaction to Policy Evaluation
3) Situation Factor at the Field

Figure 6-20	Policy Evaluation

Validity & Reliability

Validity	Internal Validity : Whether the policy effect is really due to policy or other factors. That's why we need a good Research Design by checking to include all the relevant variables in the equation. External Validity : Whether your research findings can be applied in other circumstances(time, place), we call it has a external validity.
Reliability	■ When the other person apply the same methodology and same data, it should produce same empirical results. This is the foundation of Science. ■ Critical Factors of Reliability: ① Measurement Issue: Data or Questionnaire ② Sensitive Reaction of Policy Evaluation ③ Situation Factor: Complexity at the Field

Process

Finally, it may be useful to review the right process of policy evaluation. The desirable process is as follows:

1) policy objectives

2) setting criteria

3) causality inference

4) research design

5) operationalization and measurement

6) data collection, and finally

7) analysis and findings

At the final stage, you will deduce implications and recommendations based upon your findings.

| Figure 6-21 | Policy Evaluation |

Deriable Process

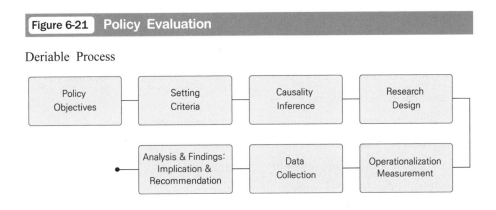

Summary and Conclusion

In this chapter, we elucidated the theory and methodologies of policy analysis and policy evaluation. To ensure effective policy making, we need to learn the skills and methodologies to analyze the complex dimensions of public policy. Especially in this chapter, we highlighted the foresight skills which are the most updated technologies of policy analysis. Obviously, it is the most critical issue for effective policy making. They will provide the most technical methodologies to provide useful analysis and information which will be greatly important for the top policymaker to make a decision most effectively. As we enter into a knowledge society, 'know-how' is much more important than 'know-what' as you can easily find out the information such as 'what' issue through the search engine of your smartphone.

First, for policy analysis, we highlighted the important theories and methodological skills of the quantitative approach as well as the qualitative approach. For the quantitative approach, we reviewed theoretical modeling, regression analysis, and simulation with sensitivity analysis. For the qualitative approach, we reviewed the Classic Delphi, Policy Delphi, Cross Impact Analysis, and Feasibility Analysis. And we also reviewed the crucial issues of Policy Design, Policy Criteria, and Comprehensive Policy Design Table and its Analytic components for effective policy analysis.

Second, for policy evaluation, we highlighted the important theories and methodological skills of experiment and non-experiment(called Statistics). We addressed the issues including
1) What are the true conditions for the true experiment?
2) What are causal inference and its conditions?
3) What are validity and reliability? And finally
4) What is the desirable process for effective policy evaluation?

Key Point!

1. Policy Analysis and Scientific Inquiry

▶ Scientific inquiry is very important. The public officials should always carry out a scientific inquiry: Why does this problem keep happening? What are the fundamental causes and reasons to affect this result? And what are the causal mechanisms between the independent variables and the dependent variable?

▶ A good analysis takes the following steps: 1) Having Academic Puzzles by asking what are the most fundamental problems in your society? 2) Setting up Hypotheses. 3) What is the Causal Relationship between the variables? 4) What is your Theoretical Argument? 5) What is our Empirical Model? 6) Perform Analysis using quantitative and qualitative methodologies: we will focus on these skills especially in this chapter. And finally, 7) Findings: what are the policy implications, and what would be your most feasible recommendations?

2. Analytical Tools(1): The Foresight Methodology as a Policy Analysis

i) Quantitative Methodology

▶ This is the most effective way to analyze. Three approaches stand out: 1) Theoretical Model, 2) Regression Analysis, 3) Simulation: Sensitivity Analysis.

1) Theoretical Modelling: Theoretical modeling means to confirm the causal relationship that would affect the policy outcomes by deducing the factors from the previous theories and articles and to clarify the causal relationship between policy measures(independent) and policy outcomes(dependent).

2) Regression Analysis: Regression analysis is the statistical method to estimate the direction and size of the relationship between the independent and dependent variables.

3) Simulation: Simulation or Sensitivity analysis is also very useful to give valuable information to the top decision-maker. By changing the value of the assumptions underlying the uncertainty, it is very helpful for decision making. The examples include the sensitivity analysis of public amusement parks whether to invest in it or not.

ii) Qualitative Methodology

1) Brainstorming:

These qualitative methods may start with Brainstorming. A good example was the Cuban Missile Crisis Strategic Solution with Brainstorming.

The flowing chart of the decision making at the time was like this: The first dominating idea of Surgical Strike → Future Possibilities with Surgical Strike(Futures Wheel) → What would then be the other Alternatives to Preventing the 3rd Nuclear World War(Decision Tree) → Naval Blockade(Final Policy Making).

2) Scenario Planning:

After Brainstorming you may proceed to Scenario Planning. For example, to predict what will be the future scenario for the smart cities: two positive scenarios of the favorable and ecological pattern: 1) horizontal extension of the city, 2) respond actively to climate change; and the other two negative scenarios of declining: 3) declining collapse of the city, and 4) respond passive to climate change, that is 1) prosperity with coexistence, 2) existing problems of machinery city, 3) dividing cities, and 4) declining and doomed collapse.

3) Policy Delphi

Policy Delphi has three features: 1) selective anonymity, 2) polarized statistical processing, and 3) intentionally framed the structured conflicts. The steps for Policy Delphi are as follows:

1. Select carefully Delphi participants & designs questionnaire
2. Analyze the results of the responses
3. Repeat the process
4. Ignite the structured conflicts
5. Finalize report of findings

4) Cross Impact Analysis

The Cross Impact Analysis is an excellent methodology to show the following features of the forecasting event:

1. Direction
2. Strength
3. Time Difference

5) Feasibility Analysis

Feasibility Analysis helps the Top-decision maker to forecast the expected result such as whether the policy bill will be passed or not. The Feasibility factors are as follows:

※ Feasibility Factors:
Key Actors
1. Direction: Plus or Minus
2. Available Resources
3. Relative Impact

iii) Analytical Elements

▶ Reflexivity: It is policy criteria for the highest value of humanity. It is the realization of human dignity at the individual level and the realization of a trustful and mature society at the community level. The specific measuring index are 1) Appropriateness, 2) Adequacy, 3) Equity and 4) Responsiveness.

▶ Democracy: It becomes more critical as society changes from bureaucracy to New Governance. Accordingly, we need a Deliberative

Democracy more than ever before. This criterion has two critical elements: 1) Procedural Democracy (Legality, Validity), and 2) Substantive Democracy (Degree of Participation, Deliberation, Consensus).

▶ Productivity: It is policy criteria to select the most effective and efficient policy option. The components are 1) Efficiency, and 2) Effectiveness. The methods to analyze these criteria are 1) Cost-Benefit Analysis, and 2) Cost-Effectiveness Analysis. The most popular methodology to compare the benefit and the cost, called PV(Present Value) and NPV(Net Present Value) are as follows.

$$\text{Present Value (PV)} = \frac{F}{(1+r)^t}$$

F: Financial Value at future time t, r: discount rate from the industrial bank

$$\text{Net Present Value (NPV)} = \sum_{t=0}^{t=T} \frac{B_t}{(1+r)^t} - \sum_{t=0}^{t=T} \frac{C_t}{(1+r)^t}$$

▶ Feasibility: It is policy criteria to assess the real feasibility of a certain policy alternative. It has six empirical components: 1) Political feasibility, 2) financial feasibility, 3) social feasibility, 4) Administrative feasibility, 5) legal feasibility, and 6) technical feasibility. The total feasibility index can be calculated as follows:

▶ Total Feasibility Index=Direction*Available Resources*Relative Impact

3. Analytical Tools(2): Policy Evaluation

i) Features

▶ Policy Evaluation has the following three features:
1) Focus: It focuses on the Performance: output, outcome & impact

2) Criteria: Efficiency, Effectiveness, Equity, Responsiveness, Adequacy(timing, degree), Appropriateness(value, trend, the spirit of the time: time, speed, uncertainty, VUCA)

3) Careful Assessment: It will find out whether it is necessary for government intervention, if any, then what kinds of intervention is needed?

ii) Method and Experiment

▶ Policy Evaluation needs to have a scientific method. It has two methods: experiment and non-experiment. The true experiment needs two conditions: 1) Random Assignment: Experiment group and Control group based on the randomization principle; otherwise, we would have a selection bias. 2) Treatment: And check the before and after Treatment. We call it the policy or program effect. That the logic and rationale of the Experiment.

iii) Causal Inference

▶ The three conditions for causal inference are:
- Time Precedence: The independent variable should occur before the dependent variable.
- Covariance: There should exist correlation and covariance between the independent and dependent variables.
- Control Third Variable: You should control the other background characteristics not to have a spurious or confounding effect.

The regression equation is like this:
$$\text{Income}_i = \alpha + \beta_1(\text{Education}) + \beta_2(\text{SES: Father or Mother's Wealth}) + \varepsilon_i$$

iv) Validity & Reliability

▶ Validity: To ensure the real causal relationship, you need to understand the concept of validity and reliability. Validity is asking that your finding is really ensuring the real cause.

▶ Reliability: Reliability refers to the situation whether your research or evaluation is really reliable. If it does, we call it reliability or reproducibility. The factors that reduce reliability are as follows:

    1. Measurement Issue: Data or Questionnaire
    2. Sensitive Reaction to Policy Evaluation
    3. Situation Factor at the Field

v) Process

▶ Finally, it may be useful to review the right process of policy evaluation. The desirable process is as follows: 1) policy objectives, 2) setting criteria, 3) causality inference, 4) research design, 5) operationalization and measurement, 6) data collection, and finally 7) analysis and findings. At the final stage, you will deduce implications and recommendations based upon your findings.

| Figure 6-22 | Discussion Question: Policy Evaluation |

Effective
Policy
Making

- Discuss about policy analysis methods, What are the quantitative methods? What are the qualitative methods?
- Discuss about Regression and Sensitivity Analysis, Also discuss about Brainstorming, Scenario Planning, and Feasibility Analysis, Show the Concrete Example of your policy issue.
- What would be the most useful method to apply & explain your policy issue?
- Discuss about policy evaluation methods, What is true experiment? What are the conditions for the true experiment?
- Discuss about how to apply True Experiment to your policy issue:
1) For example, H.E.I(Health, Employment, Industry 4.0)Team, if you have a policy program boosting employment, discuss how to evaluate the specific program;s effectiveness: Think about Before and After; Experiment Group and Control Group.
2) For the Vision Team: Discuss how would you use the Scenario Planning Method to clearly mapping out the Vision & Strategy of 2030 or 2040.

Figure 6-23	**Team Assignment for Implementation Stage**

Effective Implementation	* Team Assignment for Implementation Stage: • Each team presents the current AS-IS and TO-BE strategic solutions: • Especially with the five variables of leadership, technology, management, attitude, open cultures and the other substantive factors of funding, capacity, silos, resistance to change, and infrastructure. • For example, if you are the member of the H.E.I(Health, Employment, Industry4.0) Ministry Team, consider these issues: What are the problems? How to handle the employment issues, such as the unemployment risks faced by the Industry 4.0. How to restructuring industrial structures by utilizing Smart technologies and Smart e-government. • If you are the Vision Team, especially focus on the strategic solutions using Smart government, industrial structures, and digital technologies.

Chapter 7

POLICY IMPLEMENTATION AND ACTION

The Action Approach for Effective Policy Making

Without a feasible implementation with a desirable action agenda,

Effective policy making would be futile.

✎ ››› Objectives

The purpose of this chapter is to elucidate the implementation and action plan for Smart Policy Framework 4.0. It is to provide a new action perspective of effective policy making by reviewing the theories and action plan for policy implementation.

First, it will highlight the implementation and action approach to effective policy making by comparing the perspectives of Traditional Bureaucracy and New Governance.

Second, it will highlight the Conditions of Successful Implementation by illustrating 1) Strong Leadership and Commitment, 2) Clear Policy Design, 3) Policy Target Groups, and 4) Capacity Building.

Third, it will highlight that success and failure are actually in the same continuum.

Finally, by comparing the case of the US Oakland project and Korean economic policy making, it will highlight the five conditions for policy success and effective policy framework.

The Implementation and Action Approach to Effective Policy Making: Traditional Bureaucracy and New Governance

Definition

Without implementation, there would be no realization of activities and no results whatsoever. Therefore, policy implementation is one of the most critical areas to ensure effective policy making. In a traditional bureaucracy, people thought that once the policy decision is made, policy realization will be automatically followed, which is not true. But now people know better than that, namely, policy implementation is another area to ensure policy success. To have a better implementation, we need to have a checkpoint for the effective implementation stage, like the appropriate resources, dedicated staff members, and the rightful time schedules. That's why we need good foresight skills, clear goal setting, and policy analysis.

Figure 7-1   Policy Implementation

Bureaucracy & Governance

1) Definition:

   Without Implementation, there would be no realization activities, no results what soever.

2) Policy Implementation and Effective Policy Making: Future Foresight

Policy Implementation & Future Foresight

Traditional Bureaucracy	New Governance
Once the policy decision is made, people thought that the policy realization will be automatically followed.	Policy implementations is another issue. For effective implementation we need to consider implementation issues even at policy making stage with a foresight technology.

The Conditions of Successful Implementation

For effective and successful implementation, we need the following conditions.

Strong Leadership and Commitment

We need strong leadership and commitment. It includes strong support from the top policymaker and support from policy-related groups. As we will see later, the Korean economic success would not be possible if there were no such strong and committed leadership of President Park Chung Hee who set the cornerstones of a strong industrial and technological foundations to the Korean economy.

Clear Policy Design

With strong leadership, we need an effective policy design. The vision and goal should be simple and clear to the people. The policy design should be valid in which policy initiatives should have a causal impact on the development. The policy design should be consistent regardless of the changes in the political regime.

Policy Target Groups

If strong leadership and good policy design is a supply factor, the demand factor is also very important. That's why we need a good education and an awakening program. To have good communication, we should take into account the following non-compliance factors, though. They include

ⓐ Unclear Communication

ⓑ Insufficient Budget

ⓒ Improper Policy, Overburden, and

ⓓ Distrust of Authority

Capacity Building

If the staff members have enthusiasm and dedication, the implementation will be successful. That is why we need HRD and Attitude Change and that is why we need Education and Training for Capacity Building.

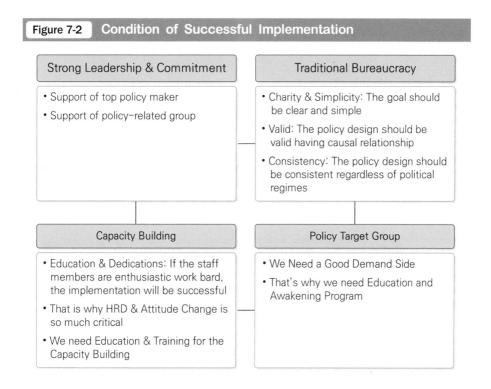

Figure 7-2 Condition of Successful Implementation

Strong Leadership & Commitment
- Support of top policy maker
- Support of policy-related group

Traditional Bureaucracy
- Charity & Simplicity: The goal should be clear and simple
- Valid: The policy design should be valid having causal relationship
- Consistency: The policy design should be consistent regardless of political regimes

Capacity Building
- Education & Dedications: If the staff members are enthusiastic work bard, the implementation will be successful
- That is why HRD & Attitude Change is so much critical
- We need Education & Training for the Capacity Building

Policy Target Group
- We Need a Good Demand Side
- That's why we need Education and Awakening Program

Success and Failure

For effective implementation, we need to know that success and failure is a continuous process. It is not just a matter of quantity but the matter of quality as well. Hence, success and failure are lying on the continuum dimension. It is very important to comprehend the following three failure concept:

1) **Non-Implementation:** there was no implementation at all.

2) **Unsuccessful Implementation:** Implementation initiated, but there was no output.

3) **Policy Failure:** There was an output. But there was no significant outcome or effect.

Figure 7-3 Success and Failure

Success & Failure

① The Success and failure is a Continuous concept
② It is not just a matter of quantity but the matter of quality as well
③ Hence, the success and failure is a Continuum dimension

Hogwood & Gunn	Non-implementation & Unsuccessful Implementation	Levin & Ferman
• Type of Failure: Non-Implementation Policy Failure	1) Non-Implementation: There was no implementation at all 2) Unsuccessful Implementation imitated, but there were no output 3) Policy Failure: There were output, But not significant outcome or effect	• Policy Failure 1) Serious side-effects 2) Delray of timing 3) Successive financial budget

Classical Administrative Model

The classical administrative model is based upon the following three important premises:

Politics-Administration Dichotomy

This principle is argued by W. Wilson who initiated the classical administration theory in his famous article(1887), "The Study of Administration." He was the 28th President of the United States and also served as the president of Princeton University. He was the founder of the contemporary public administration.

He emphasized the dichotomy principle to protect the administration from the notorious political nepotism prevalent in the 1880s in the United States. He stated that "Politics and Administration are two different domains. Policy making is the domain of politics while Administration is the domain of implementation. Therefore, Public Administration is an independent area, possessing unique principles and professionalism."

Hierarchical Bureaucracy

The classical administration is based on the hierarchical structure of bureaucracy. This format of steep and rigid structure also implies that policy decisions are made at the Top and what Staff members should do is to only follow the boss's direction.

Efficiency First

The classical administration is based on the Taylorism that highlighted "Efficiency is the only the best supreme value," which may not be true in the modern policy economy. The only efficiency with a hurried decision oftentimes results in a larger disaster. Taking a proper procedure and trustful and mature reflexivity are indispensable in the contexts of the modern policy economy which are volatile, uncertain, complex, and ambiguous dynamics.

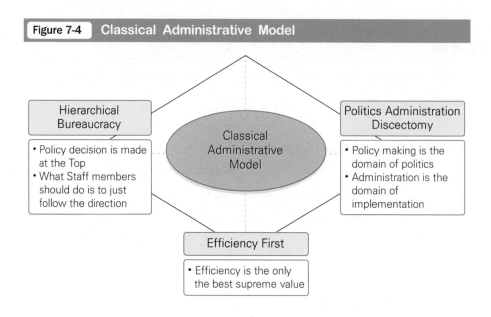

Figure 7-4 Classical Administrative Model

Classical Implementation Model

The classical implementation model, therefore, builds up the following three important pillars.

Wilson's Public Administration

As mentioned, public administration is based on W. Wilson's Politics-Administration Dichotomy. The dichotomy strictly argued that politics is policy making and administration is policy implementation.

Weber's Bureaucracy

Public administration is also based on M. Weber's Bureaucracy Theory. The bureaucracy theory argued the principle of division of labor, hierarchical decision making, and legal & document-oriented administration to ensure efficiency.

Taylor's Scientific Management

Public administration is also based on F. Taylor's Scientific Management. The scientific management argued that there exists one best way of efficiency rule if we keep the rule of time and motion principle which is called scientific management.

The Classical implementation model seems wonderful in appearance. But in fact, this classical model has some fundamental flaws as follows:

1. **Policy Making and Implementation is Homogeneous;**
   Rather they are Heterogeneous.

2. **After Policy Making, Implementation will not be carried out Uni-directionally;**
   Rather, they are very Interactive in a two-way direction.

3. **Implementation will not be carried out Mechanically and Automatically the decisions made by Policy Makers; Rather, they are very Complexity and Circulative.**

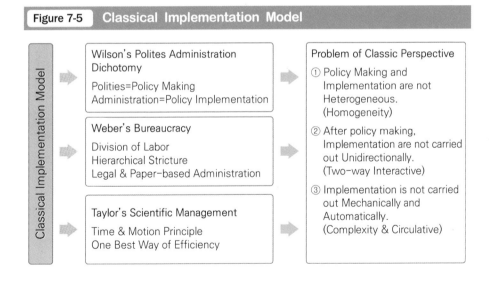

Figure 7-5 **Classical Implementation Model**

Classical Implementation Model

Wilson's Polites Administration Dichotomy

Polities=Policy Making
Administration=Policy Implementation

Weber's Bureaucracy

Division of Labor
Hierarchical Stricture
Legal & Paper-based Administration

Taylor's Scientific Management

Time & Motion Principle
One Best Way of Efficiency

Problem of Classic Perspective

① Policy Making and Implementation are not Heterogeneous. (Homogeneity)

② After policy making, Implementation are not carried out Unidirectionally. (Two-way Interactive)

③ Implementation is not carried out Mechanically and Automatically. (Complexity & Circulative)

Modern Implementation Model

The Modern implementation model has gone through the evolutionary development from the first generation to the third generation.

First Generation

First Generation focused on a specific Policy Implementation case:

1. Identify the characteristics of policy implementation.
2. Research focuses on specific policy implementation programs.

Second Generation

Second Generation focused on 2-3 Policy Implementation cases and found that:

1. Implementation strategy should be different from policy to policy, from time to time.
2. Attempts to explore theory to explain this kind of changing paradigm.

Third Generation

Third Generation focused on several Policy Implementation cases to develop the Analytical Framework for Policy Implementation. The Third Generation began to identify three Essential Features:

1. **Causal Complexity**
2. **Dynamics in Nature**
3. **Diversity in the Fields**

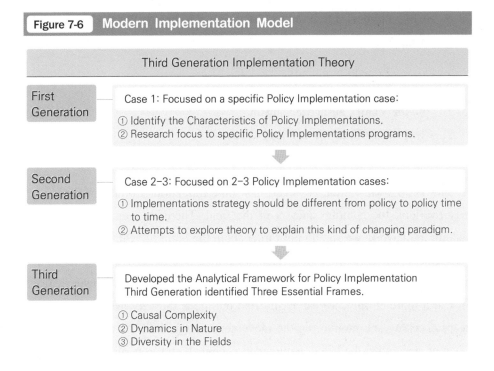

Figure 7-6 Modern Implementation Model

Third Generation Implementation Theory

First Generation — Case 1: Focused on a specific Policy Implementation case:

① Identify the Characteristics of Policy Implementations.
② Research focus to specific Policy Implementations programs.

Second Generation — Case 2-3: Focused on 2-3 Policy Implementation cases:

① Implementations strategy should be different from policy to policy time to time.
② Attempts to explore theory to explain this kind of changing paradigm.

Third Generation — Developed the Analytical Framework for Policy Implementation
Third Generation identified Three Essential Frames.

① Causal Complexity
② Dynamics in Nature
③ Diversity in the Fields

Top-Down Model

The modern implementation model has developed in three ways: The Top-Down Model, the Bottom-Up Model, and Integrated Model.

First of all, the Top-Down Model prefers a top-down approach which in many cases is appealing to the developing countries. In fact, it was the Korean economic success model from the 1960s to the 1980s. Let's look at the features of the model:

1. **Policy decisions should be based on the Valid Causal Mechanism.**
2. **Policy contents should be Clear.**
3. **Competent and Dedicated Staff**
4. **Strong and Committed Leadership**

5. **Stable Political Environment in which the Policy Priority will not be changed.**

Top-Down Model has the following strengths:

1. **Provide Valid Causal Mechanism**
2. **Clear Policy Contents & Policy Goals**
3. **Good Checklist for Effective Policy Making**

The Top-Down Model, however, has some limitations in modern times as it may overlook the complex factors in the field. Therefore, for effective policy making framework, we should not forget about the point of "Our answers exist at the Field." In fact, when we study the Park Chung Hee Leadership and his model, it may seemingly look like a Top-Down Model in the first place. However, if we look at it more closely, we can easily find out, he is the very leader who always keeps checking and monitoring the movements in the field. As a matter of fact, when he developed the heavy equipment, chemical, and iron and steel industries in Pohang, Woolsan, and Changwon areas of South Korea, he himself designed, implemented, and monitored with close consultation with his expert staff members. This kind of attitude to check it by himself seems to be cultivated and embedded in his earlier military careers. He was an Army General before he became President. On the battlefields, as you know, the most effective leader does not fail to overlook the field sites. It is not theory; it is a real fight.

| Figure 7-7 | Top Down Model |

| Top-Down Approach | • Policy decisions should be based on Valid Causal Mechanisms.
• Policy contents should be Clear.
• Competent and Dedicated Staff.
• Strong and Committed Leadership.
• Stable Political Environment in which the Policy Priority will not be changed. |

| Top Policy Maker | Clarify the Intention | Each step of the Project will be specifically Concretized | Compare Implementation Performance with Original Goal | Field-line Staff Officers |

Strengths	Limitations
① Provide Valid Causal Mechanism ② Clear Policy Contents & Policy Goals ③ Good Checklist for Effective Policy Making	• In Modern time, we should also consider some Complex factors in the field.

▌ Bottom-Up Model

Bottom-Up Model highlights the interrelationship among the key stakeholders such as bureaucrats and local government agencies. It has the strengths to better explain the implementation network in the field and can provide more effective implementation strategies that can be established in the field. However, this approach could ignore the Macro Political-Economic Factors at the National Level, which oftentimes could be more disastrous in the developing countries.

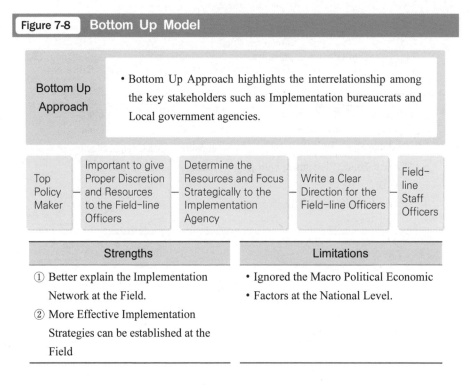

| Figure 7-8 | Bottom Up Model |

Bottom Up Approach

• Bottom Up Approach highlights the interrelationship among the key stakeholders such as Implementation bureaucrats and Local government agencies.

| Top Policy Maker | — | Important to give Proper Discretion and Resources to the Field-line Officers | — | Determine the Resources and Focus Strategically to the Implementation Agency | — | Write a Clear Direction for the Field-line Officers | — | Field-line Staff Officers |

Strengths	Limitations
① Better explain the Implementation Network at the Field. ② More Effective Implementation Strategies can be established at the Field	• Ignored the Macro Political Economic • Factors at the National Level.

Integrated Model

Academic efforts have been converted to complement the strengths and weaknesses of Top-down and Bottom-up Models and present the Integrated Model. Sabatier, for example, stated that the downward and the upward approach should be mutually integrated and Elmore, similarly, argued that the forward and backward approach should be mutually integrated.

Matland specifically argued that we need to consider the Specific Implementation Strategies considering Ambiguity and Conflict at the Field. Winter, furthermore, suggested to consider the following specific factors:

1) **Policy Making Characteristics**
2) **Policy Implementation Characteristics:**
   a) **Behavior Patterns of Organization**
   b) **Behavior Patterns of Staff members**
   c) **Behavior Patterns of Policy Target Group**

| Figure 7-9 | Integrated Model |

• Academic efforts have emerged to complement the strengths and weaknesses of Top-down & Bottom-up approaches.

Sabatier	Elmore	Matland	Winter

• The downward and the upward approach should be mutually integrated.	• The forward and backward approach should be mutually integrated.	• Specifically argued that we need to consider the Specific Implementation Strategies considering Ambiguity and Conflict at the Field.	• Suggested the following specific factors to consider:
			1) Policy Making
			2) Policy Implementation:
			  a) Behavior Patterns of Organization
			  b) Behavior Patterns of Staff members
			  c) Behavior Patterns of Policy Target Group

Successful Implementation

Successful implementation should have the following criteria: Goal Achievement, Time and Budget, and Smoothness.

Goal Achievement
This criteria is asking, "How much has the policy achieved its original intended goals?"

Time and Budget
This criteria is asking, "Is it Timely? And was it a reasonable Cost?"

Smoothness
This criteria is asking, "How smoothly the policy was achieved?"

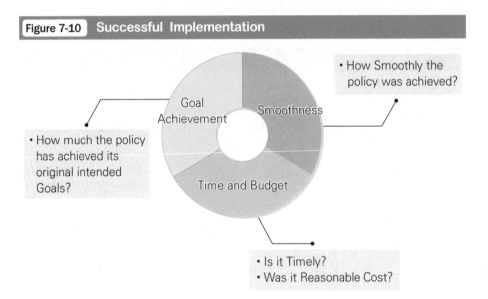

Figure 7-10　Successful Implementation

Having scanned all theories and models of successful policy implementation, now let's examine the real stories of the USA and Korea to comprehend a better idea of an effective policy framework.

Case Story: USA

Pressman and Wildavsky wrote a very important book named, "Implementation"(1973) and they analyzed the implementation failure of the Oakland Project which invested 23 Million USD and was aimed at producing 2,200 new job opportunities. But three years later, the policy evaluation illustrates that the Project turned out to be a total failure, only creating less than a mere 10 jobs with spending only 3 million dollars. To their astonishment, there was no artificial corruption or bribery. What they found as the failure points are:

1. Too many Participant Agencies

2. Too many Veto Points

3. Frequent Replacement

4. Lack of Technical Validity Causal mechanism

This story vindicates our conclusion of policy success in a strong way; the successful conditions for policy success are in these five points:

1. **Strong and Committed Leadership**
2. **Clear Vision:** The Vision and Goal of the policy should be Clear.
3. **Causal Mechanism:** Policy Making should be based on the Valid Causal Mechanism(Technical Validity).
4. **Competent and Dedicated HRD:** We need Capacity Building with Attitude Change.
5. **Stable Political Environment:** We don't want our policy priority faltering soon after the new President seats the chair.

Figure 7-11	The Case of USA: Oakland Project

Lessons & Implications

> Case Story:
> US EDA, Oakland Project investing 2,300 (10thousand) $ and producing 2200 new job opportunities. But turned out to be less than 3 Mill and only 10 new job. Pressman & Wildavsky, Implementation(1973) analyzed the failure as follows:

Failure Factors	Success Features
① Too many Participant Agencies	① Strong and Committed Leadership
② Too many Veto Points	② Clear Vision
③ Frequent Replacement	③ Causal Mechanism
④ Lack of Technical Validity & Causal mechanism	④ Competent and Dedicated HRD
	⑤ Stable Political Environment

With this tentative conclusion in mind, in the following section, we will analyze the Korean case of economic success by searching into an effective policy framework.

Analyzing the Korean Case of Economic Policy: Effective Policy Framework

Some Economic Profile

Korea is the 12th largest economy from the GDP scale. Among the large population of countries over 50 million, it is the 7th economic power in the world and became an OECD member nation. This is not just from a quantitative perspective.

Qualitatively, Korean E-government has been evaluated as the world's best for the last six consecutive years. Incheon international airport has been evaluated as the world's best for the last 14 years. Recently, Korean agile response with a high level of digital capacities saved thousands of lives from the COVID-19 crisis, evaluated and lauded as a remarkable success case from the world-renowned global-scale foreign presses abroad, Washington Post, New York Times, Wall Street Journal, and the BBC to name a few.

The Korean manufacturing industries, along with high-tech digital structures have a very sound and strong foundation, from automobiles, shipbuilding, nuclear power plants to Semiconductor, ADSL, 5G, IoT, AI, Bio, Drone, Self-driving cars, and Big data systems.

How could Korea achieve its economic success, called the miracles of the Han River, within a relatively short time period, about 50 to 70 years or so?

Experiencing a harsh and severe Korean War for three years from 1950 to 1953, more than 6 million casualties, Seoul and every other city in Korea turned down to ashes. Millions and thousands of people were dying from absolute poverty and hunger. Korea was the unique country that could transform into an ODA donor country graduating from the ODA recipient country after World War II. Every year a lot of public officials from the developing countries all over the world came to the Sungkyunkwan(SKKU) university of Korea(Samsung Foundation) to learn the world's best E-government and local innovation through the full scholarship of KOICA program which is the ODA implementation agency in Korea.

What happened in Korea, then? How Korea could possibly accomplish its economic miracles and what kinds of policy strategies Korea has employed during this period?

How is effective policy making massively determined the success and progress of Korea?

What were the lessons and implications cast on the other developing nations?

Analysis and Findings

Three items and findings stand out for explaining the successful Korean economic policies.

1) There was a focus, objective and goal

In the Korean economic policy case, first of all, there was a focus, objective and clear goal. The focus was a high-speed, high-tech digital network and digital government. The objective was a strong and effective infrastructure and the goal was effective policy making and smart e-Government.

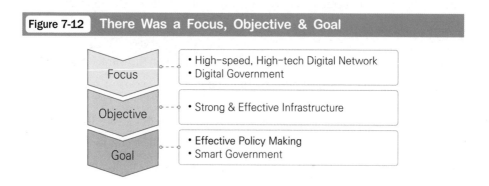

Figure 7-12   There Was a Focus, Objective & Goal

Focus
- High-speed, High-tech Digital Network
- Digital Government

Objective
- Strong & Effective Infrastructure

Goal
- Effective Policy Making
- Smart Government

2) There was a Strategic Approach

In the Korean economic policy case, there was a strategic approach for effective policymaking. Here, it is very important to ask in each stage of economic and industrial policy:

1) which policy?

2) whose initiation? and

3) attaining a strategic policy set

For the specific policy criteria, it is critical to analyze the industrial spillover effect, technological spillover effect, and market spillover effect. Then, we will attain more effective policy making.

| Figure 7-13 | There was a Strategic Approach: For Effective Policy Making |

3) There was a clear pattern of Korean economic strategy for a decade-wise

Finally, in the Korean economic policy case, decade-wise, there was a clear pattern of economic strategy. Roughly speaking, in the 1960s, it was a light-wear industry such as shoes, clothes, and wigs utilizing relatively cheap labor resources. In the 1970s, Korea transformed its industrial structures into a heavy-equipped industry such as automobile, shipbuilding, chemical, and steel and heavy machinery industry. In the 1980s, Korean economy again transformed into more electronic and digital-switch technology; in the 1990s, information superhighway, high-speed internet, and broad-band project; in the 2000s, electronic government and commerce using ADSL, WiBro, and DMB; and in the 2010s, now we are highlighting about the advanced smart technologies such as AI, Big data, IoT, Self-driving Car, Drone, Bio in the 4th industrial revolution.

| Figure 7-14 | Decade-wise There Was a Strategy: Pattern of Korean Effective Policy Making |

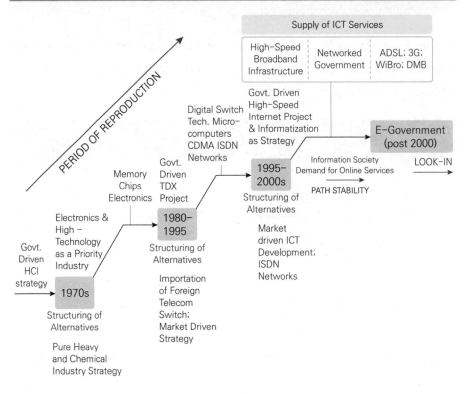

Having a Clear Vision and Strategy: Effective Policy Making

It is very useful, at this moment, to review the roadmap of Korean economic strategy: Having a clear vision and strategy. The vision is to make an advanced smart society 4.0 with high creativity and trust. The goals are

1) citizen life enrichment

2) economic vitalization

3) government efficiency

4) social security, and

5) smart infrastructure improvement

And the strategy is to make a strong ICT infrastructure by focusing on the positive aspects so that Korea highlights an effective policy making to make a more strong and great nation with a foundation of smart governance 4.0.

Figure 7-15 Having a Vision & Strategy: Effective Policy Making

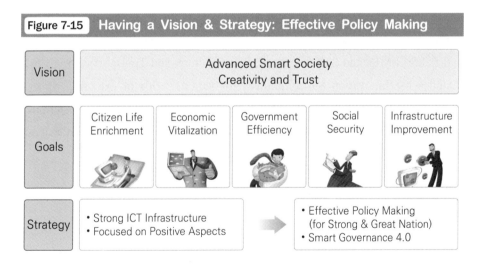

Korean Smart e-Governance System: Effective Policy Making

In Korea, the Presidential Committee on the 4th industrial revolution established under President deliberates on the agenda related to the smart e-government and the initiatives related to the 4th industrial revolution. The Korean government established the Presidential Committee on the Fourth Industrial Revolution (PCFIR) and started to drive consensus-building for changes.

The PCFIR deliberates upon and coordinates important policy matters of the development and acquisition of new science and technology, including artificial intelligence (AI) and data technology, as well as new industries and services necessary for Korean society's adaptation to the 4th Industrial Revolution.

Consists of 24 members, including one chairperson, The Committee's inaugural members include the Chairperson, the Science Advisor to the President as the administrator, the private sector experts, and the ministers of participating departments (i.e., Science and ICT; Trade, Industry, and Energy; Employment and Labor; SMEs and Startups; Land, Infrastructure, and Transport). The PCFIR includes the Innovation Subcommittees for various fields of expertise, Special Subcommittees for in-depth discussions on specific policy issues, and Committee secretariat. The PCFIR consists of three Innovation Subcommittees on Science and Technology, Industry and Economy, and Social system.

Korean Smart e-Government Strategic Governance System

Presidential Committee on the 4th industrial revolution

| Figure 7-16 | Presidential Committee on the 4th industrial revolution |

Co-chairman: Prime Minister, Civilian Expert

Members(24): Science Advisor to the President as the administrator, the private sector experts, and the ministers of participating departments (Science and ICT; Trade, Industry and Energy; Employment and Labor; SMEs and Startups; Land, Infrastructure and Transport)

Presidential Committee on the 4th industrial revolution

PCFIR SECRETARIAT

Innovation Sub-committee

Special Sub-committee

Ministry of Science and ICT

| Science and Technology | Industry and Economy | Social System |

| Digital Health care | Smart City | ... |

Prospects future, analyzes issues

Carry out innovation polices

Share Policy direction
Modify Policies

Finds key task areas, supports implementation

| Ministry of strategy and finance | Ministry of SMEs and Startups | Ministry of SMEs and Startups | ... | Ministry of Employment and Labor | Ministry of Health and Welfare |

| Ministry of the interior and Safety | Ministry of Land, infrastructure and ransport | | | Local Government |

Vision and Strategy

The vision of Korean National Information is to realize advanced knowledge and information society that ensures the convenience and safety of the people according to the spirit of creativity and trust. Here, 'creativity' means to create a new value-added and to improve the efficiency of each sector of national society by the creative use of Smart ICT devices. 'Trust' means to create an environment of sustainable information promotion based on sound and healthy information culture. Ultimately, it aims to contribute to the realization of a leading & advanced nation, which is a strong and great nation.

To accomplish this supreme vision, the Korean government has established the following four practical strategies based on creativity and confidence unlike in the past: 1) utilization-oriented, 2) convergence-oriented, 3) active response for information dysfunction, and 4) public-private collaborative e-governance system. The vision and strategy of the Korean National Information are drawn as the following figure:

The Vision and Strategy of Korean Smart e-Governance

Figure 7-17 Korean Smart e-Government Strategic Governance

Strategies	Improving Quality of Life	Self-Innovating Government with Digital Capacities	Establishing Transparent Society	Nationwide Intelligent Infrastructure
Goal	Online Government	Intelligent Government	Smart and Warm e-Government	Network Government
Vision	Global Leader in e-Government Developing Sustainable Future			

* Source: Ministry of the Interior and Safety(2020)

The overall Smart e-governance scheme has been working very successfully and can be evaluated in the most positive way. The Korean Smart e-Governance system has been functioning very effectively by establishing a new vision and direction at the strategic level so that the Korean Smart e-governance policy and 4th industrial revolution related policy will be strongly activated to realize the strong and great nation in which each citizen can fully accomplish their own vision and goal.

Critical Success Factors: Korean Smart e-Government Policy

The critical success factors of the Korean Smart e-Government policy can be analyzed as follows:

1) Strong Information Infrastructure based on economic development especially in the electronics, semiconductor, and heavy-equipped industries, which was early pursued by the strong and committed leadership of President Park Jung Hee.

2) Consistent ICT Infrastructure Projects and Smart e-Government Initiatives uninhibited by the changes of the political regimes.

3) Combination of Supply(Government-drive) and Demand(Social needs based on People's education and awareness) Strategies.

4) Combination of Top-down Government Drive and Incentive-based Public-Private Partnership.

5) Strong Promotion Committee supported by the national highest level of Governance, such as President and Prime Minister.

Figure 7-18 Korean Model: Lessons & Implications

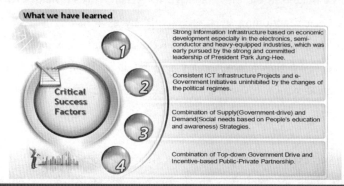

Figure 7-19 Korean Model: Lessons & Implications

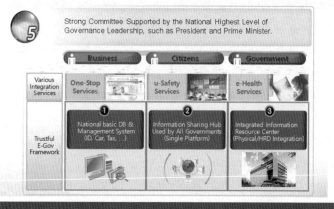

Strategic Solution & Action Agenda for the Developing Countries

For effective policy making, there are at least five major variables to consider:

1) capacity building

2) silos: lack of collaboration

3) resistance to change

4) power and infrastructure

5) funding.

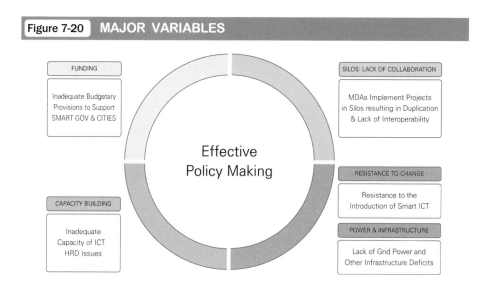

Figure 7-20 MAJOR VARIABLES

Also, for effective policy making, we need to comprehend five critical steps to policy success:

1) strong and committed leadership

2) technology factor

3) institutional factor

4) attitude factor, and

5) culture factor

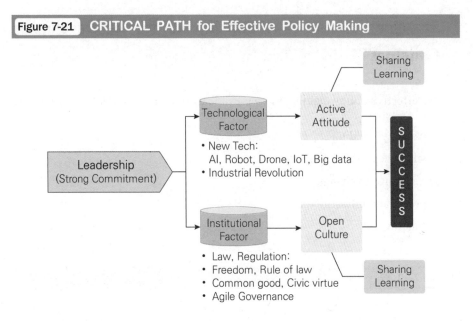

Figure 7-21 CRITICAL PATH for Effective Policy Making

Then, my suggestions to the developing countries are two by two matrix models of strategic solution for their development and innovation. The strategic diagram is shown as below. It presents a working sheet to analyze from the current status(As-Is) to the innovation state(To-Be). The horizontal axis shows the five critical paths and the vertical axis illustrates the five major variables that usually become impediments to the innovation of the developing nations. This strategic model will be a very effective and powerful tool-kit for those nations for their innovation and development.

Figure 7-22	STRATEGIC SOLUTION

		LEADERSHIP	TECH.	MGMT.	ATTITUDE	CULTURE
FUNDING	As is		§		§	§
	To Be		§		§	§
CAPACITY	As is	§	§		§	§
	To Be	§	§		§	§
SILOS	As is	§	§		§	§
	To Be	§	§		§	§
RESISTANCE TO CHANGE	As is					
	To Be					
INFRA STRUCTURE	As is			§	§	§
	To Be					

Summary and Conclusion: Effective Policy Framework

In this chapter, we elucidated the implementation and action plan for smart policy framework 4.0. It was to provide a new action perspective of effective policy making by reviewing the theories and action plan for policy implementation.

First, we highlighted the implementation and action approach to effective policymaking by comparing Traditional Bureaucracy and New Governance.

Second, we highlighted the Conditions of Successful Implementation by illustrating

1) Strong Leadership & Commitment
2) Clear Policy Design
3) Policy Target Groups and
4) Capacity Building

Third, we highlighted the success and failure are actually in the same Continuum dimension.

Finally, by comparing the case of the US Oakland project and Korean Economic Policy Making, it will highlight the five successful conditions for policy success and effective policy framework.

The five successful conditions were as follows:

1. Strong and Committed Leadership
2. Clear Vision: The Vision and Goal of the policy should be Clear.
3. Causal Mechanism: Policy Making should be based on the Valid Causal Relationship(Technical Validity).
4. Competent and Dedicated HRD: We need Capacity Building with Attitude Change.
5. Stable Political Environment

Key Point!

1. Implementation & Action Approach to Effective Policy Making

▶ Without Implementation, there would be no realization activities, no results whatsoever. Therefore, policy implementation is one of the most critical areas to ensure effective policy making .

2. Success and Failure

▶ For effective implementation, we need to know that success and failure is a continuous concept. It is not just a matter of quantity but the matter of quality as well. There exist three cases, lying on the continuum.

    1) **Non-Implementation:** there was no implementation at all.

    2) **Unsuccessful Implementation:** Implementation initiated, but there was no output.

    3) **Policy Failure**: There was an output. But there was no significant outcome or effect.

3. Classical Implementation Model

▶ The Classical implementation model, therefore, builds up the following three important pillars.

1) Wilson's Public Administration

▶ Public administration is based on W. Wilson's Politics-Administration Dichotomy. The dichotomy strictly argued that politics is policy making and administration is policy implementation.

2) Weber's Bureaucracy

▶ Public administration is also based on M. Weber's Bureaucracy Theory. The bureaucracy theory argued the principle of division of labor, hierarchical decision making, and legal & document-oriented administration to ensure efficiency.

3) Taylor's Scientific Management

▶ Public administration is also based on F. Taylor's Scientific Management. The scientific management argued that there exists one best way of efficiency rule if we keep the rule of time and motion principle which is called scientific management.

4. Modern Implementation Model
1) Top-Down Model

▶ Top-Down Model prefers a top-down approach which in many cases is appealing to the developing countries. In fact, it was the Korean economic success model from the 1960s to the 1980s. Let's look at the features of the model:

① Policy decisions should be based on the Valid Causal Mechanism.
② Policy contents should be Clear.
③ Competent and Dedicated Staff
④ Strong and Committed Leadership
⑤ Stable Political Environment in which the Policy Priority will not be changed.

2) Bottom-Up Model

▶ Bottom-Up Model highlights the interrelationship among the key stakeholders such as implementation bureaucrats and local government agencies.

3) Integrated Model

▶ Academic efforts have been converted to complement the strengths and weaknesses of Top-down & Bottom-up Models and present the Integrated Model.

5. Case Story: USA

▶ Pressman & Wildavsky wrote a very important book, named "Implementation" (1973) and they analyzed the implementation failure of the Oakland Project which invested 23 Million US $ and was aimed at producing 2,200 new job opportunities. But three years later, the policy evaluation illustrates that the Project turned out to be a total failure, only creating less than a mere 10 jobs with spending only 3 million dollars. To their astonishment, there was no artificial corruption or bribery. What they found as the failure points are:

1. Too many Participant Agencies
2. Too many Veto Points
3. Frequent Replacement
4. Lack of Technical Validity Causal mechanism

▶ This story vindicates our conclusion of policy success in a strong way; the successful conditions for policy success are in these five points:

1. Strong and Committed Leadership
2. Clear Vision: The Vision and Goal of the policy should be Clear.
3. Causal Mechanism: Policy Making should be based on the Valid Causal Mechanism(Technical Validity).
4. Competent and Dedicated HRD: We need Capacity Building with Attitude Change.
5. Stable Political Environment: We don't want our policy priority to keep changing soon after the new President seats the chair.

6. Critical Success Factors: Korean Smart e-Government Policy

▶ The critical success factors of the Korean Smart e-Government policy can be analyzed as follows:

1) Strong Information Infrastructure based on economic development especially in the electronics, semiconductor, and heavy-equipped industries, which was early pursued by the strong and committed

leadership of President Park JungHee.

2) Consistent ICT Infrastructure Projects and Smart e-Government Initiatives uninhibited by the changes of the political regimes.

3) Combination of Supply(Government-drive) and Demand(Social needs based on People's education and awareness) Strategies.

4) Combination of Top-down Government Drive and Incentive-based Public-Private Partnership.

5) Strong Promotion Committee supported by the national highest level of Governance, such as President and Prime Minister.

7. Strategic Solution & Action Agenda for the Developing Countries

▶ For effective policy making, there are at least five major variables to consider: 1) capacity building, 2) silos: lack of collaboration, 3) resistance to change, 4) power and infrastructure, 5) funding.

▶ Also, for effective policy making, we need to comprehend five critical steps to policy success: 1) strong and committed leadership, 2) technology factor, 3) institutional factor, 4) attitude factor, and 5) culture factor.

▶ Then, my suggestions to the developing countries are two by two matrix models of strategic solutions for their development and innovation. The strategic diagram is shown as below. This strategic model will be a very effective and powerful tool-kit for those nations for their innovation and development.

Figure 7-23 STRATEGIC SOLUTION

		LEADERSHIP	TECH.	MGMT.	ATTITUDE	CULTURE
FUNDING	As is		§		§	§
	To Be		§		§	§
CAPACITY	As is	§	§		§	§
	To Be	§	§		§	§
SILOS	As is	§	§		§	§
	To Be	§	§		§	§
RESISTANCE TO CHANGE	As is					
	To Be					
INFRA STRUCTURE	As is			§	§	§
	To Be					

Figure 7-24	Discussion Question: Policy Implementation

| Effective Policy Making | • Discuss about the USA Oakland Project, What are the failure factors?
• What are the five critical success factors of implementation?
• Discuss about the South Korean Economic Development case, What are the CSF factors?
• What is the Traditional Implementation Approach?
• What is the modern Implementation Approach?
• What are the five critical variables for GCC 2040 Process Viewpoint?
• What are the five major issues for the Smart Government Strategy? |

Chapter 8

The 4ᵀᴴ INDUSTRIAL REVOLUTION & LEADERSHIP

The Leadership Approach for Effective Policy Making

The 4th Industrial Revolution is not just an industrial revolution.

It will change everything; even it will define who we are.

⟫⟫ Objectives

The purpose of this chapter is to elucidate the theory and strategies to actively respond to the 4th Industrial Revolution. Facing this turbulent new environment, the government should respond with a new attitude, leadership, and governance.

First, it will highlight the leadership approach to effective policy making under the new ear of the 4th Industrial Revolution.

Second, it will highlight the definition, value stream, and strategic issues facing the 4th Industrial Revolution.

Finally, it will highlight the National Re-design with Smart Policy Framework 4.0. The BluePrint will show the government innovation which will integrate politics, economy, capital, and citizens in a new way.

The Leadership Approach to Effective Policy Making: The 4th Industrial Revolution

As the 21st century unfolds, we are living in a chaotic and turbulent society. Speed of thought becomes very important as information and knowledge is the most critical factor of national competitiveness. To achieve national competitiveness, thereby building a great and strong nation, effective policy making is crucial to achieving government innovation and national transformation.

The unfolding of the 21st century has brought the world into a new and different turn. It's

an era of time, speed, and uncertainty. The 4th Industrial revolution is characterized by volatility, uncertainty, complexity, ambiguity. Under these times of turbulence, innovation is crucial to achieving the transformation of governance under society 4.0. To achieve innovation and transformation, effective policy making is indispensable.

Such swirl of information revolution requires an unsullied evaluation of the existing governance model and its operating system. In particular, up until now, the bureaucratic model has led to modern development and its operating system is largely dependent on the steep, rigid, and hierarchical system based on command and control.

The modern way in this uncertain era should be based on the Smart paradigm. The Smart paradigm highlights the clear policy goal setting, effective policymaking & analysis with quantitative and foresight methodologies, new government reform, and updating the legal framework. The goal is to make a more slim, agile, and flexible policymaking system with an aid of more smart and innovative technologies to make a more open & transparent culture.

The 4th Industrial Revolution

Definition

The 4th Industrial revolution is like a wind. Wind, although invisible, we can feel and touch it. From the national level, the nation who embarks on the wind and upgrades national competitiveness will be the winner of its destiny. The 4th Industrial revolution is a new civilization paradigm that will integrate and converge the physical, digital, and biological areas into one system. It will be the society of super-network, super-intelligence, and super-prediction with foresight which will change and transform all the forms of human life.

Figure 8-1	SMART PARADIGM 4.0			

Index	1st Industrial Revolution	2nd Industrial Revolution	3rd Industrial Revolution	4th Industrial Revolution
Age	1780's	1900's	1970's	2016-
Technology	Steam Engine	Electric/ Electronics	ICT/ PC	Smart ICT/ Convergence AI, IOT, Big Data, Clouding, Mobile
Innovation	Steam Engine Harnessing	Division of Labor Using Electricity	Computer Equipment	Smart ICT/ Creative Economy
Means of Production	Machine	Massive Production/ Ford System	Computerization	Artificial Intelligence/ Deep Learning
Core Energy	Coal	Coal/ Oil	Nuclear Energy	Bio Energy/ Natural Energy
Transportation &Communication	Train/ Telegraph	Automobile/ Airplane/ TV	Express Train/ Internet	Aerospace Industry
Means of Communication	Books/ Newspapers	Telephone/ TV	Internet/ SNS	IoT/Clouding Big Data

Value Streaming

The 4th Industrial revolution will create a value system with effective policymaking. As shown below, the new value creation model will dictate to make a stronger and greater nation by integrating from agenda-setting, policymaking, policy analysis, policy implementation, policy evaluation, and change. All the knowledge streams and value streams will be converged. From asset investment, information, and knowledge creation & sharing will change the Platforms. That's why we need a new capacity building by incorporating this new stream of value and knowledge.

Figure 8-2	Analytical Model for the Industrie 4.0 in Germany

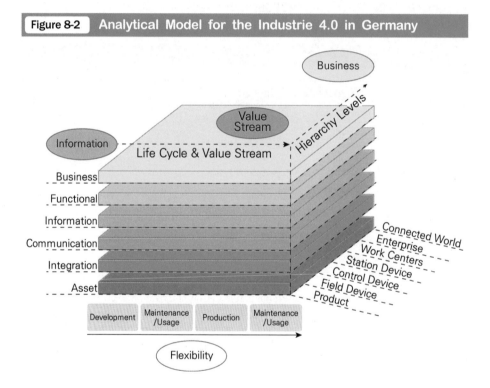

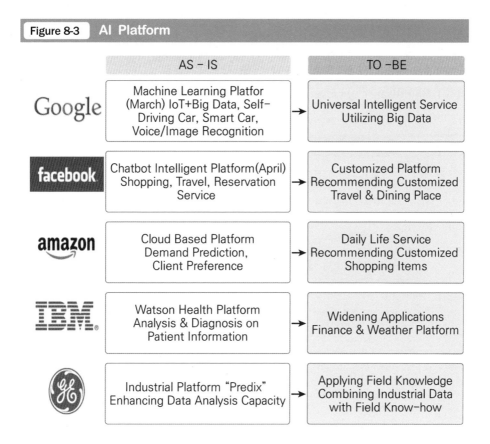

Figure 8-3 AI Platform

How to Prepare for the 4th Industrial Revolution?

The WEF report predicts that by 2030, the World GDP will be increased by the amount of 15 Trillion U.S. Dollars with the value creation of the 4th industrial revolution. But 70 thousand jobs will disappear with only 20 thousand job creations, meaning that at least 50 thousand jobs will be changed. How should the government be responsible for these situations like mass-scale unemployment?

The key items are as follows:

1) The World Is Changing
2) We need to Re-define the Role of Technology: Connectivity with Big Data, AI Platform

3) Human is the Key

4) Retraining of the Existing HRD

5) Preparing for the Future HRD, and

6) Significance of Government Role

Figure 8-4 **Keyword & Strategy of 4th Industrial Revolution**

- KEY WORD: Super-Connectivity, Super-Intelligence, Perfect-Prediction
- 4th: IT + AI, Big Data, IOT, BIO Convergence (3nd: PC, Computer-Oriented)
▶ Wearable Robot, Iron Man, Subminiature Robot, AI Robot, Drone, Industrial intelligence

Benchmarking	Government Role
Germany • Industry 4.0 • Government-led Smart Manufacturing System • Connecting Industry to Industry • 2020: 10.9 Billion Euro • IOT. CPS(Cyber Physical System). Standardization. Big data → Self Diagnosis & Control → innovation	**Big Governance** • Presidential Leadership + Private Experts
USA • Smart Manufacture Leading Company(SMLC) • Smart Standardization • R&D for Super Industry	**4th Industrial Revolution Strategy Committee** • Policy Strategy • Smart Manufacturing Standardization & R&D • Industrial Restructuring • Labor Structure • Education & Training

▌ Agile Governance with Responsible and Responsive Leadership

As we mentioned earlier, Harvard John F. Kennedy School of Government started a new policy research center named Future Society. Echoing J. F. Kennedy's famous vision, "on the edge of a new frontier," the research center embarked on the new research about NBIC(Nano, Bio, Information, Cognitive brain science). They highlighted that we need a new vision of effective policy making under the vision of society 4.0.

The government model has evolved through a different stage, namely Government 1.0, 2.0, 3.0, and now we are facing a new governance model. As mentioned, we are facing a new and different turn, more chaotic and turbulent society, characterized by volatility, uncertainty, complexity, and ambiguity. Industrial Revolution 4.0, artificial intelligence, NBIC, and the new virus Crises with other social disasters approaching us as a heightened uncertainty, we have to consider seriously the new agile governance model with a more responsible and responsive leadership.

Figure 8-5 Davos Forum 2017

World 2020	2020 Davos Agenda	Davos Initiatives

4th Industrial Revolution

Protectionism Indigenous Democracy

Global Risk
* Climate Change
* Mass Destructive Weapon
* Refugees Crisis

Global Depression Increasing Uncertainty

Leadership of Responsive &Responsibility

* Active Response to the problems faced
* Responsibility to provide vision & solutions
* Establishing future-oriented policy making system

◆ Leadership Challenges:
① Revitalizing Global Economy
② More Opening World Market
③ Preparing 4th Industrial Revolution
④ Strengthen International Cooperation

① The Future of Consumption
② the Future of Digital Economy
③ The Future of Economic Growth
④ The Future of Education, Gender, & Work
⑤ The Future of Energy
⑥ The Future of Natural Resources Security
⑦ The Future in Financial and Monetary System
⑧ the Future of Food Security and Agriculture
⑨ The Future of Health and Health Care
⑩ The Future of Information and Entertainment
⑪ The Future of Trade and Investment
⑫ the Future of Infrastructure and Development
⑬ The Future of Mobility
⑭ The Future of Production

* Revised from the World Economic Forum(Global Agenda Council), "Future of Gov ernment"(2020).

The New Governance Model in the era of the 4th Industrial Revolution

The 4th Industrial Revolution changed the way the government operates based on the principle of super-connectivity, super-intelligence, and super-prediction.

The new governance system enables us to provide customized services and personalized services by utilizing Big data, AI, and IoT technologies, going much beyond the simple use of PC and Electronic devices in the past. It also enables real transparent administration and effective policy making by utilizing Big data systems.

However, there exist some concerns and negative aspects. For instance, social inequalities
could have been much deeper under Society 4.0 as the information gap and digital divide could be much widening. Thus, we need to deeply analyze and understand the dysfunctions as well as the functions that the political process of the 4th Industrial Revolution might result in.

Then, what would be the new governance model in the era of the 4th Industrial Revolution?

In the path-breaking research,『The Future of Government: Lessons Learned from around the World』, the World Economic Forum, or called Davos Forum, highlighted that the governance in the era of the 4th industrial revolution should be based on the FAST(Flatter, Agile, Streamlined, Tech-Savvy) model.

The new governance in the era of the 4th Industrial Revolution should be:

1) **Flatter government** that can solve the social problems quickly through the
   flexible and horizontal policy making structure. To this end, the

government should promote the following elements:

(1) **Citizen engagement**: Increased public participation in the policy process by using SNS and Mobile devices.

(2) **Administrative efficiency**: Improve administrative efficiency by reducing unnecessary administrative procedures and red-tape.

(3) **Decision-making process**: Horizontal policy making by performing Scientific policy analysis with Big data.

(4) **Collaboration**: Solving social problems by using inter-governmental, and cross-sectoral network system.

2) **Agile government** that can mobilize resources and staff to solve social problems quickly.

3) **Streamlined government** that can utilize technological innovation. Rather than down-sizing mechanically, it should use an innovative way to improve efficiency by utilizing the e-Government model and its BPR system.

4) **Tech-Savvy government** that can equip the future-oriented technological capacity. Tech-Savvy the government should not only improve technical capacity but include the policy redesign, legal framework supporting the new governance system as a whole.

Figure 8-6	Government Model in the Age of the Fourth Industrial Revolution

FAST MODEL

Feature	Content
Flatter	* Flatter government that can solve the social problems quickly through the flexible and horizontal policy making structure. To this end, the government should promote the following elements: 1) Citizen engagement: Increased public participation in the policy process by using SNS and Mobile devices. 2) Administrative efficiency: Improve administrative efficiency by reducing unnecessary administrative procedures and red-tape. 3) Decision-making process: Horizontal policy making by performing Scientific policy analysis with Big data. 4) Collaboration: Solving social problems by using inter-governmental, and cross-sectoral network systems.
Agile	* Agile government that can mobilize resources and staff members to solve the social problems quickly. To this end, the government should promote the following elements: 1) Network government: The government solves the social problem using public and private networks, but the branch will be dissolved when the mission is completed. 2) Capacity Building: The government should promote capacity building to cultivate the professional knowledge worker. 3) Intelligent government: The government should establish an intelligent network.
Streamlined	* Streamlined government through technological innovation. Rather than down-sizing mechanically, it should use an innovative way to improve efficiency by utilizing the e-Government model and its BPR system.
Tech-Savvy	* Tech-Savvy government with a future-oriented technological capacity. The tech-Savvy government should not only improve technical capacity, but include the policy redesign, legal framework supporting the new governance system as a whole.

* Revised from the World Economic Forum(Global Agenda Council), "Future of Gov ernment"(2020).

National Re-design with Smart Policy Framework 4.0

As shown below, we need a national reinvention and redesign with the blueprint of smart policy framework 40, discussed earlier. The Blue Print will show the government innovation which will integrate politics, economy, capital, and citizens in a new way. This new vision would have two pillars: one with a creative mindset, and the other with a structural approach like new governance. In other words, the mindset and system should be integrated in a new way. For the mindset, new leadership should be strong but with an accountable attitude that will transform the national system with an effective policy strategy. And for the system part, we need to create a new growth engine facing the 4th Industrial Revolution with the spirit of new partnership and collaboration among government, business, and civil society.

Figure 8-7 NATIONAL REDESIGN: SMART POLICY FRAMEWORK 4.0

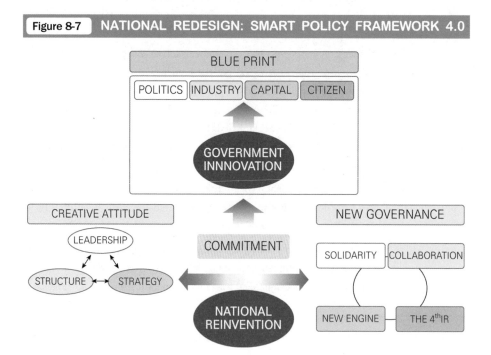

▌ Summary and Conclusion: Smart Policy Framework 4.0

In this chapter, we elucidated the theory and strategies to actively respond to the 4th Industrial Revolution. Facing this turbulent new environment, the government should respond with a new attitude, leadership, and governance.

First, we highlighted the leadership approach to effective policy making under the new ear of the 4th Industrial Revolution.

Second, we highlighted the definition, value stream, and strategic issues facing the 4th Industrial Revolution.

Finally, we highlighted the National Re-design with Smart Policy Framework 4.0. The Blue Print will show the government innovation which will integrate politics, economy, capital, and citizens in a new way. This new vision would have two pillars: one with a creative mindset, and the other with a structural approach like new governance. The new leadership should be strong but with an accountable attitude who will transform the national system with an effective policy strategy. The new leadership also needs to create a new growth engine facing the 4th Industrial Revolution with the spirit of new partnerships and collaboration.

Key Point!

1. The Leadership Approach to Effective Policy Making: The 4th Industrial Revolution

▶ As the 21st century unfolds, we are living in a chaotic and turbulent society. Speed of thought becomes very important as information and knowledge is the most critical factor of national competitiveness.

▶ The modern way in this uncertain era should be based on the Smart paradigm. The Smart paradigm highlights the clear policy goal setting, effective policymaking & analysis with quantitative and foresight methodologies, new government reform, and updating the legal framework. The goal is to make a more slim, agile, and flexible policymaking system with an aid of more smart and innovative technologies to make a more open & transparent culture.

2. The 4th Industrial Revolution

Definition

▶ The 4th Industrial revolution is a new civilization paradigm that will integrate and converge the physical, digital, and biological areas into one system.

▶ It will be the society of super-network, super-intelligence, and super-prediction with foresight which will change and transform all the forms of human life.

Value Streaming

▶ The 4th Industrial revolution will create a value system with effective policymaking. The new value creation model will dictate to make a stronger and greater nation by integrating from agenda-setting, policymaking, policy analysis, policy implementation, policy evaluation, and change. All the knowledge streams and value streams will be converged.

Agile Governance with Responsible and Responsive Leadership

▶ We are facing a new and different turn, more chaotic and turbulent society, characterized by volatility, uncertainty, complexity, and ambiguity.

▶ Industrial Revolution 4.0, artificial intelligence, NBIC, and the new virus Crises with other social disasters approaching us as a heightened uncertainty, we have to consider seriously the new agile governance model with a more responsible and responsive leadership.

The New Governance Model in the era of the 4th Industrial Revolution

▶ The new governance in the era of the 4th Industrial Revolution should be:

1) Flatter government that can solve the social problems quickly through the flexible and horizontal policy making structure.

2) Agile government that can mobilize resources and staff to solve social problems quickly.

3) Streamlined government that can utilize technological innovation. Rather than down-sizing mechanically, it should use an innovative way to improve efficiency by utilizing the e-Government model and its BPR system.

4) Tech-Savvy government that can equip the future-oriented technological capacity. The tech-Savvy government should not only improve technical capacity but include the policy redesign, legal framework supporting the new governance system as a whole.

National Re-design with Smart Policy Framework 4.0

▶ We need a national reinvention and redesign with the blueprint of smart policy framework 40, discussed earlier. The Blue Print will show the government innovation which will integrate politics, economy, capital, and citizens in a new way. This new vision would have two pillars: one with a creative mindset, and the other with a structural approach like new governance.

NATIONAL REDESIGN: SMART POLICY FRAMEWORK 4.0

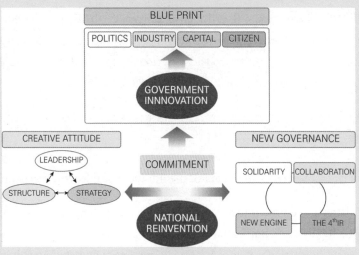

| **Figure 8-8** | **Discussion Question: Smart Policy Framework** |

| Effective Policy Making | • What is the 4th Industrial Revolution? How is it compared with the previous industrial revolutions?
• What if we do not appropriately respond the challenges of new technologies and globalization such as the Pandemic of COVID-19 Crisis.
• How do you compare the national strategy od Industry 4.0 in Germany, USA, and South Korea?
• What would be the most appropriate model for your country? And Why?
• What is the Value Creation Model?
• What are the three conditions for effective policy making: People, Process, Product? Discuss it using the terminology of Direction, Agility and Resilience by keeping in mind that Agility means speed and flexibility. |

| Figure 8-9 | Team Assignment for Implementation Stage |

| Effective Implemen-tation | * Team Assignment for Implementation Stage:
• Each team presents the current AS-IS and TO-BE strategic solutions:
• Especially with the five variables of leadership, technology, management, attitude, open cultures and the other substantive factors of funding, capacity, silos, resistance to change, and infrastructure.
• For example, if you are the member of the H.E.I(Health, Employment, Industry4.0) Ministry Team, consider these issues: What are the problems? How to handle the employment issues, such as the unemployment risks faced by the Industry 4.0. How to restructuring industrial structures by utilizing Smart technologies and Smart e-government.
• If you are the Vision Team, especially focus on the strategic solutions using Smart government, industrial structures, and digital technologies. |

SUMMARY AND CONCLUSION
Policy Implications and Recommendation for Effective
Policy Making

A real insight into the future is seeing what is invisible.

>>> Objectives

KEY FINDINGS: LESSONS & RECOMMENDATIONS

PART I POLICY DESIGN: EFFECTIVE POLICY MAKING & SMART POLICY FRAMEWORK

1. Strong & Great Nation: Policy Criteria

What would be the policy criteria that a strong and great nation should follow? To put it another way, what are the most critical criteria of good governance? The policy criteria for good governance are composed of efficiency, democracy, and reflexivity.

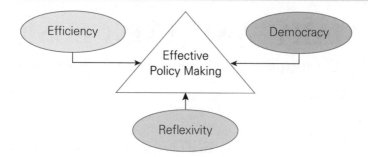

| Figure 9-1 | New Policy Theory for New Governance |

■ New Governance promotes the dimensions of democracy and efficiency at the policy at the same time by institutionally ensuring the participation of various stakeholders.

First efficiency dimension. The strong and great nation should be strong and efficient. It should perform effective policymaking. From the standpoint of smart e-Government, the efficiency dimension has four elements:

1) One, non, any stop portal government
2) Paperless and building-less government with cost reduction
3) clean and transparent government with zero corruption
4) digital neural government with knowledge management.

Second democracy dimension. The strong and great nation is a democratic nation. From the political and process standpoint, democracy is valuable and indispensable. It indicates not only political participation by the means of election and voting but more importantly policy participation by using digital government in the routine daily life. Therefore, this kind of democracy has two elements:

1) e-Policy with digital participation in the policy process
2) e-Politics with digital voting, digital congress, and digital legislation.

Thirdly, the reflexivity dimension. The strong and great nation should be reflexive. Reflexivity is a philosophical term. It refers to a supreme vision that a nation-state could realize. For instance, it means a society in which human dignity will be strictly observed, therefore, the individual citizen could freely actualize self-esteem and self-realization. In a nutshell, it is a trustful and mature society in which citizens can freely discuss social issues or public agenda using the public space in the smart e-Government. It is the highest dimension of effective policy making.

2. Recommendations

1) Perform the Check Points for Policy Quality Control

For an effective policy making government need to have a tool-kit for policy quality management. To ensure policy success, the effective policy making should have a checkpoint for each stage of the policy process

The checkpoints are as follows:

For effective policy planning,

- Have you Identified the true nature(issue) Finding of the Problem?
- Would the problem require government intervention; Is it inevitable?
- Have you checked and thoroughly investigated the previous/similar policy cases?
- Have you identified and listened carefully to the related target population or groups?

For effective policy making,

- Did you make a choice with your best option?
- Have you checked the resources necessary for the policy: Is it enough?
- Have you checked the related agencies and taken prior consultations with them?
- Have you checked and followed the legal procedures?
- Have you set up the PR Plan?

For an effective policy announcement,

• Did you take consultation and coordination with your related parties?

For an effective policy implementation,

• Did you consistently maintain the policy priority?
• Have you strategically positioned the authorities and resources required for policy implementation?
• Have you monitored the responses of the policy target group from time to time and respond aptly?
• Did you perform monitoring at the midpoint of the policy implementation such that policy implements according to the original purport?

For an effective policy evaluation,

• Do you realize your original policy goal?
• Do you set up the rewards and incentives(positive as well as negative) based upon policy evaluation?
• Do you make a document as a nice lively policy case and try to get some policy implications and policy learning.

2) Build up a new capacity building

To achieve the vision of a strong and great nation, mentioned above, we need a new capacity building for effective policy making.

For this purpose, some key agenda of a capacity-building should be:

1) Identify "fundamental problems" faced in your society.
2) Perform evidence-based policy analysis and policymaking
3) Also, learn the foundation of policy science with Smart e-Government, e-Transformation, and Attitude change for the behavioral perspectives.

3) Initiate attitude change(Institutional Level)

The most major negative attitudes in the developing countries are as follows:

1) Red-Tape(Formalism)

2) Misplacement of Goals and Means

3) Easy-going Attitude

4) Nepotism

5) Sectionalism(Silos)

6) Dependence Too Much on Boss Authority

7) Trained Incapacity, and

8) Resistance to Change

To overcome these obstacles, at a personal level, we need to be armed with clear professionalism and positive psychology. At the cultural level, we need to perform attitude change, from old analog thinking to more digital entrepreneurship, from past-oriented minds to a more future-oriented initiative, and from public administration bureaucratic mind to a more new public management innovation.

For the organization level, we need to perform effective policy management including effective agenda-setting and policymaking, and effective implementation & evaluation. Lastly, for the technical level, we need a strong ICT infrastructure and smart government foundation in which digital governance with knowledge creation and learning will be most beautifully flourished.

4) Initiate attitude change(Personal Level)

Most of all, for yourself, do the attitude change. It will give you great fortune and success. You will be getting rich, more healthy, and happy. Here are some tips for the change.

ⅰ) Perform Block+Deep!

Block+Deep means, 1) Block out any external noisy and stressful minds; and 2) Make a Deep Change by entering into your deep Consciousness level.

Stay calm and stillness. And notice that you are Consciousness in essence. The external world is a reflection of your belief and conviction. If your mindset has been changed, your outcome will be changed accordingly.

ii) Raise a Question-type Affirmation!

The question-type Affirmation never fails to find your answer and execute it to the end without much resistance. That's how our brain system works. Hence, let's perform and keep constantly raising a question-type Affirmation such as:

- **Why am I   so successful?**
- **Why am I   so effective and strong?**
- **Why am I   getting rich?**
- **Why am I   so attractive?**

iii) Have a Strong Conviction and Confidence!

There exists a clear common characteristic among the persons who possess a great fortune. Great wealth and happiness are following from your achievements. Find and notice those common characteristics such as:

- **Focusing on the Positive Aspects**
- **Having Gratitude Feelings**
- **Great Confidence**
- **Joyful Attitudes**
- **Pouring the Best Efforts before God's Decision & Judgment**

If you possess a strong conviction, you will achieve great success. Strong belief gives you great confidence, then again leading to a strong conviction. Therefore, if you have a great conviction, you will always be the winner. The strong conviction commands your brain and will achieve your goal without any resistance by attracting, like a powerful Magnet, all the possible means, and opportunities around you.

iv) Find your Pure Consciousness!

You have your Pure Consciousness or True Self within your Mind and Consciousness: Shining and Awakened, Stillness with Awareness, and Empty but full of Wisdom and Loving force. Your life essence is shining vividly within your Mind and Consciousness. It is not the thing being evaded or falling out.

ⅴ) Change your channels!

Change the channels of your Present Consciousness, from noisy and asking small ego minds to calm & stillness, and empty & silence. Also, change the channels of your Sub Consciousness, from boring, dull, and sleepy to a clear, aware, and awakened mind. We call this Practice as a Mindfulness Exercise.

- **Stay Calm, Stillness, and Silence**
- **Notice There is a Clear Awareness within Your Consciousness**
- **A Deeper and Strong Conviction will Transform Yourself.**
- **It will also enable you to Identify your True Self.**

5) Derive the Strategic Solution & Action Agenda

Let's now return to our topic of national competitiveness for the developing countries.

For effective policy making, there are at least five major variables to consider:

1) capacity building

2) silos: lack of collaboration

3) resistance to change

4) power and infrastructure

5) funding

Also, for effective policy making, we need to comprehend five critical steps to policy success:

1) strong and committed leadership

2) technology factor

3) institutional factor

4) attitude factor, and

5) culture factor

After understanding these two sets of components, perform to analyze the two by two matrix model of strategic solution for their development and innovation.

The strategic diagram is shown as below. It presents a working sheet to analyze from the current status(As-Is) to the innovation state(To-Be). The horizontal axis shows the five critical paths and the vertical axis illustrates the five major variables that usually become impediments to the innovation of the developing nations.

This strategic model will be a very effective and powerful tool-kit for those nations for their innovation and development.

Figure 9-2 STRATEGIC SOLUTION

		LEADERSHIP	TECH.	MGMT.	ATTITUDE	CULTURE
FUNDING	As is					
	To Be					
CAPACITY	As is					
	To Be					
SILOS	As is					
	To Be					
RESISTANCE TO CHANGE	As is					
	To Be					
INFRA STRUCTURE	As is					
	To Be					

6) Set up the Smart Policy Framework 4.0

Smart policy framework 4.0 highlights human dignity and public value in a more speedy, ethical, and efficient way. The goal in this framework is to make big data and evidence-based creative governance with effective policymaking. The strategy is three-fold: speed, wisdom, and fusion.

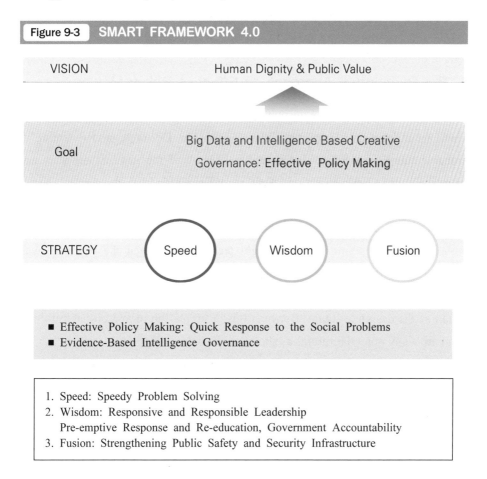

Figure 9-3 SMART FRAMEWORK 4.0

VISION — Human Dignity & Public Value

Goal — Big Data and Intelligence Based Creative Governance: Effective Policy Making

STRATEGY — Speed   Wisdom   Fusion

- Effective Policy Making: Quick Response to the Social Problems
- Evidence-Based Intelligence Governance

1. Speed: Speedy Problem Solving
2. Wisdom: Responsive and Responsible Leadership
   Pre-emptive Response and Re-education, Government Accountability
3. Fusion: Strengthening Public Safety and Security Infrastructure

First, as for speed, the new framework emphasizes the new capacity building to make quick responses to the new social problems.

Second, as for wisdom, the new framework emphasizes responsive and responsible leadership by providing pre-emptive responsive and smart systems.

Finally, as for fusion, the new framework emphasizes a more interdisciplinary and consilience approach to providing new services with a more strengthened public safety and smart security infrastructure.

PART II POLICY PARADIGM & MODELS

1. The Conceptual Approach to Effective Policy Making

For effective policy making, we need to take special attention to the future. There are at least three important futures: Probable, Desirable, and Potential. A probable future is a future that probably happens if the government does not intervene with a special action. That is the situation that the current social problems would still exist in that future. That is why we need a special action, called effective policy making by the government to solve the existing problems within society, hopefully with foresight technologies. Then the tendency was broken and the fundamental problems would be solved, and we could achieve the vision of a strong and great nation. We call this desirable situation achieving great vision as the desirable future. Between this desirable future and probable future, there are many potential futures as shown in the below diagram.

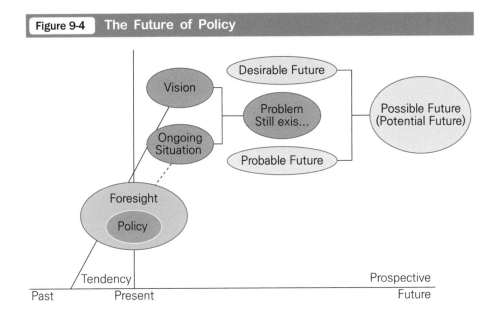

Figure 9-4   The Future of Policy

Successful Steps

Effective policy making needs to follow three critical steps with three standards: causal validity, realistic feasibility, and normative standards such as reflexivity.

1) **Causal Validity**: It means a valid Causal Relationship between policy goal and instrument. It should be effective and efficient. To ensure this dimension, we will do a cost-benefit analysis, cost-effective analysis, among others.

2) **Realistic Feasibility**: It means six feasibility criteria: political, financial, social, administrative, legal, technical feasibility.

3) **Normative Standard**: Reflexivity: It is a normative standard.

We call it the reflexivity dimension. It is the highest vision of public policy, ultimately realizing human dignity. It has two levels, one with an individual for the self-realization of each individual, the other with the community for realizing a trustful & matured society.

| Figure 9-5 | The Successful Steps of Effective Policy Making |

Criteria

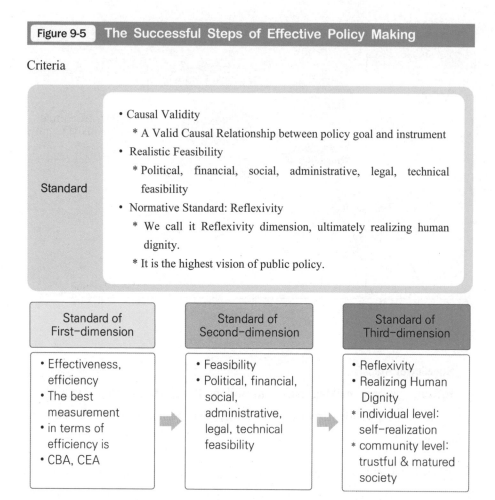

2. Recommendations

1) Perform the policy making base on the Optimal policy making Model

Definition

Policymaking is a series of government decision making to set the cornerstone for the future of the nation. Also, it is the key to effective policy making as apparent in the name.

Steps

The steps of effective policy making are:

1) problem definition and goal setting

2) prioritizing between policy goals

3) development and plan of policy alternatives

4) future foresight and comparative evaluation of alternative results, and

5) choosing the best alternatives

Figure 9-6	Steps of Effective Policy Making

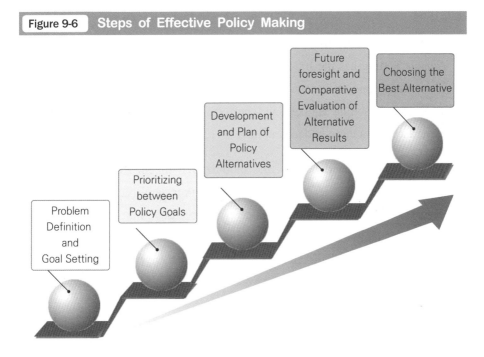

Typology

Try to comprehend the various policy making models including rational model, satisfying model, incremental model, mixed-scanning, optimal model, garbage can, policy stream, and Allison model among others. And then apply the best model to your contexts.

254 PART 4 THE 4TH INDUSTRIAL REVOLUTION

2) Understand the Process of Key Agenda Setting

Definition

Agenda Setting is an act of the government adopting social problems as a government agenda. It means that once adopted it dictates the direction of the government decision. So, it is important as it is the first step of the policy process and thereby impacting on the next policy process. Hence, it is indispensable to search for a creative policy instrument at this stage using scientific   foresight technology.

Agenda Setting Models

Agenda Setting has the following models: 1) mobilization model, 2) external initiative model, and 3) internal bureaucracy model. Hence, try to understand the logic of agenda-setting models and perform the key agenda-setting in your country based upon these understandings.

1) **Mobilization Model**: First, the mobilization model frequently occurs in developing countries, whereby the strong President wants to transform his nation into a strong state. President set up a government agenda to solve the problems of his nation. The example was the Samaeul Movement of President Park Jung Hee in Korea which saved the nation from the absolute poverty level.

2) **External Initiative Model**: Second, the external initiative model takes the steps from the outsides. In this case, civil society raises the issue from the social problem, public agenda, and to the government agenda.

3) **Internal Bureaucracy Model**: Third, the internal bureaucracy model occurs when some group of internal bureaucrats at the high level attempts to proceed with some kind of policy with a secret movement. So, it is called a type of conspiracy model, which may not be desirable.

3) Understand the Critical Policy Change Model

The following diagram shows the useful policy change model using the existing policy models: Policy Stream Model, Advocacy Coalition Model, and Policy Stage Model.

1) **Policy Stream**: First, it highlights the policy stream model which says that problem, policy, and politics flows independently before the triggering event occurs. Once the triggering event happens, the policy window will open for a new paradigm of policy.

2) **Advocacy Coalition**: When the policy window opens, it is important to understand who supports the new policy and who opposes it. The belief and resource are two critical components gauging the strength of the group, advocacy group, and anti-advocacy group which basically will tell us who is going to be the winner of the policymaking.

3) **Policy Stage**: From agenda setting, policymaking, to policy implementation and evaluation, all going through the policy stage, it is very important to elucidate this fundamental dynamics of policy change which will lead to whether success or failure.

| Figure 9-7 | Policy Change for Effective Policy Making |

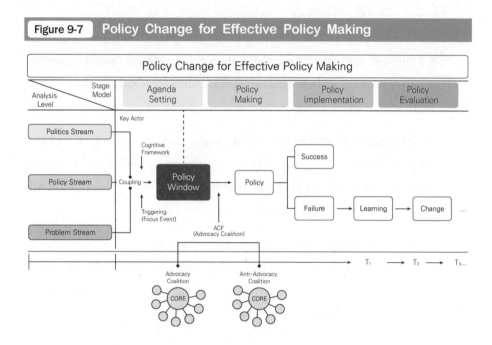

4) Understand the Logic of Policy Process Model

Policy Process starts with the basic question, who dominates the policy process: Elite or Plural group; Corporatism; Sub Government model, the Policy community, and Issue network.

It is the topic regarding the Power Model perspective: Who Governs? Or Who dominates the policy process? Therefore, try to understand the dynamics of the policy process in your country, and transform the process in a desirable way.

In doing so, it is important to understand the two faces of the policy process: one with a rational aspect, the other with a political aspect. The rational aspect consists of 1) rational policy instrument, 2) professionalism, and scientific process, while political aspect consists of 1) conflict of interests, 2) political game, and 3) political power.

Figure 9-8	Policy Process Model: Power Model

Two Faces of Policy Process

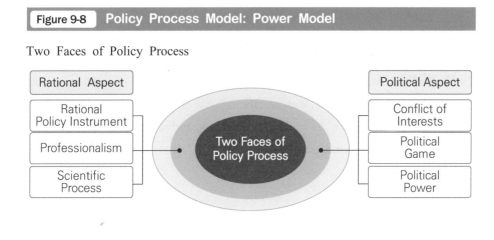

▌ PART III POLICY ANALYSIS & IMPLEMENTATION

1. Policy Analysis and Scientific Inquiry

To perform effective policy making it is critical to comprehend the fundamental methodologies of policy analysis. In other words, policy analysis is the key to the policy capacity building. If we cannot possess the working knowledge to perform the technical methodologies, we could not analyze the detailed policy problems and alternatives. Therefore, it is crucial for public officials in developing countries to gain practical knowledge to exercise statistical analysis.

Scientific inquiry is very important. The public officials always carry a scientific inquiry: Why does this problem keep happening? What are the fundamental causes and reasons to affect this result? And what are the causal mechanisms between the independent variables and the dependent variable?

An effective analysis takes the following steps:

1) Having Academic Puzzles by asking what are the most fundamental problems in your society?
2) Setting up Hypotheses.

3) What is the Causal Relationship between the variables?

4) What is your Theoretical Argument?

5) What is our Empirical Model?

6) Perform Analysis using quantitative and qualitative methodologies: we will focus on these skills especially in this chapter. And finally,

7) Findings: what are the policy implications, and what would be your most feasible recommendations?

2. Recommendations

1) Understand Policy Success & Failure is lying on a Continuum

For effective implementation, we need to know that success and failure is a continuous concept. It is not just a matter of quantity but the matter of quality as well. Hence, success and failure are lying on the Continuum dimension. It is very important to comprehend the following three failure concept:

(1) **Non-Implementation**: there was no implementation at all.

(2) **Unsuccessful Implementation**: Implementation initiated, but there was no output.

(3) **Policy Failure**: There was an output. But there was no significant outcome or effect.

2) Understand the Conditions of Successful Implementation

For effective and successful implementation, we need the following conditions.

Strong Leadership & Commitment

We need strong leadership and commitment in the first place. It includes strong support from the top policymaker and support from policy-related groups. As we will see later, the Korean economic success would not be possible if there were no such strong and committed leadership of President Park Jung-Hee who set the cornerstones of a strong industrial and technological foundations to the

Korean economy.

Clear Policy Design

With strong leadership, we need an effective policy design. The vision and goal should be simple and clear to the people. And the policy design should be valid in which policy initiatives should have a causal impact on the development. And the policy design should be consistent regardless of the changes in the political regime.

Policy Target Groups

If strong leadership and good policy design is a supply factor, the demand factor is also very important. That's why we need a good education and an awakening program. To have good communication, we should take into account the following non-compliance factors, though. They include ⓐ Unclear Communication, ⓑ Insufficient Budget, ⓒ Improper Policy, Overburden, and Distrust of Authority.

Capacity Building

If the staff members have enthusiasm and dedication, the implementation will be successful. That is why we need HRD & Attitude Change and that is why we need Education & Training for Capacity Building.

3) Understand the Conditions of Policy Success

After analyzing the US case of Oakland Project, we could find that the successful conditions for policy success are in these five points:

(1) **Strong and Committed Leadership**

(2) **Clear Vision**: The Vision and Goal of the policy should be Clear.

(3) **Causal Mechanism**: Policy Making should be based on the Valid Causal Mechanism(Technical Validity).

(4) **Competent and Dedicated HRD**: We need Capacity Building with Attitude Change.

(5) **Stable Political Environment**: We don't want our policy priority faltering soon after the new President seats the chair.

4) Have a Clear Vision & Strategy

In addition, the Korean economic success story tells us: Having a clear vision and strategy. The vision is to make an advanced smart society 4.0 with high creativity and trust. The goals are 1) citizen life enrichment, 2) economic vitalization, 3) government efficiency, 4) social security, and 5) smart infrastructure improvement. And the strategy is to make a strong ICT infrastructure by focusing on the positive aspects so that Korea highlights an effective policy making to make a more strong and great nation with a foundation of smart governance 4.0.

5) Understand the KSF of Korean Smart e-Government Policy

The key success factors of Korean Smart e-Government, with a similar vein, can be analyzed as follows:

(1) Strong Information Infrastructure based on economic development especially in the electronics, semiconductor, and heavy-equipped industries, which was early pursued by the strong and committed leadership of President Park Jung-Hee.

(2) Consistent ICT Infrastructure Projects and Smart e-Government Initiatives uninhibited by the changes of the political regimes.

(3) Combination of Supply(Government-drive) and Demand(Social needs based on People's education and awareness) Strategies.

(4) Combination of Top-down Government Drive and Incentive-based Public-Private Partnership.

(5) Strong Promotion Committee supported by the national highest level of Governance, such as President and Prime Minister.

PART IV THE 4ᵀᴴ INDUSTRIAL REVOLUTION

1. Value Streaming

The 4ᵗʰ Industrial revolution will create a value system with effective policymaking. As shown below, the new value creation model will dictate to make a stronger and greater nation by integrating from agenda-setting, policymaking, policy analysis, policy implementation, policy evaluation, and change. All the knowledge streams and value streams will be converged. From asset investment, information, and knowledge creation & sharing will change the Platforms. That's why we need a new capacity building by incorporating this new stream of value and knowledge.

2. Recommendations

1) Perform the Agile Governance with Responsible and Responsive Leadership

Harvard John F. Kennedy School of Government started a new policy research center named Future Society. Echoing J. F. Kennedy's famous vision, "on the edge of a new frontier," the research center embarked on the new research about NBIC(Nano, Bio, Information, Cognitive brain science). They highlighted that we need a new vision of effective policy making under the vision of society 4.0.

2) Understand the New Challenges

The government model has evolved through a different stage, namely Government 1.0, 2.0, 3.0, and now we are facing a new governance model. Government 1.0 was a traditional way of administration based on Max Weber's Bureaucratic model. Government 2.0 was a market approach of administration based on New Public Management. Government 3.0 was a value approach of administration based on Mark Moor's Public Value Model. Now, as mentioned already, we are facing a new and different turn, more chaotic and turbulent society, characterized by volatility, uncertainty, complexity, and ambiguity. Not only witnessing a new technological explosion but a new virus crisis like COVID-19 are presenting an unprecedented way of social life. Such a swirl of revolutionary challenges requires an unsullied evaluation of the existing governance model and its operating system. Industrie 4.0, artificial intelligence, NBIC, and the new virus Crises with other social disasters approaching us as a heightened uncertainty, we have to consider seriously the new agile governance model with a more responsible and responsive leadership.

3) Clearly Set Up the New Vision

Smart Governance 4.0 highlights a new vision of a strong and great nation with effective policy making in which government, market corporates, and NGOs are collaboratively networking with a trustful and mature manner. It also highlights government accountability more than ever before as we vividly saw in the crisis of COVID-19.

In this sense, the new framework emphasizes to clarify government's public value more clearly. Based on the smart e-government technology and more predictive policy making using foresight methodology technology, the new framework should make more efforts to meet ever heightened people's expectations of not just providing service delivery but to provide public services more efficiently, effectively, agile and responsive way. They are asking "remember me, involve me, and inspire me."

4) Perform the National Re-design with Smart Policy Framework 4.0

We need a national reinvention and redesign with the blueprint of smart policy framework 40. The BluePrint will show the government innovation which will integrate politics, economy, capital, and citizens in a new way.

This new vision would have two pillars: one with a creative mindset, and the other with a structural approach like new governance. In other words, the mindset and system should be integrated in a new way.

For the mindset, new leadership should be strong but with an accountable attitude that will transform the national system with an effective policy strategy.

And for the system part, we need to create a new growth engine facing the 4th Industrial Revolution with the spirit of new partnership and collaboration among government, business, and civil society.

Figure 9-9 NATIONAL REDESIGN: SMART POLICY FRAMEWORK 4.0

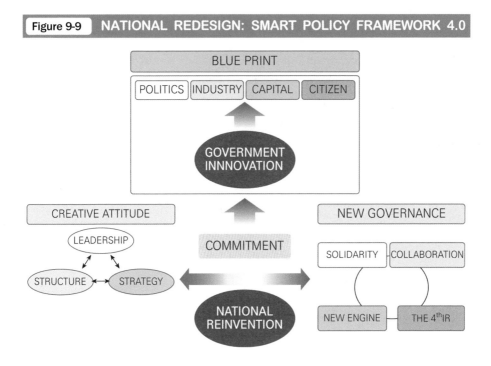

Epilogue

The unfolding of the 21st century has brought the world into a new and different turn.

The 4th Industrial revolution is characterized by volatility, uncertainty, complexity, ambiguity. Under these times of turbulence, innovation is crucial to achieving the transformation of governance under society 4.0. To achieve innovation and transformation, effective policy making is indispensable. And to achieve national competitiveness, thereby building a great and strong nation, effective policy making is crucial to achieving government innovation and national transformation.

Human beings are not the owner of the earth, nor can leave here eternally; we just stay here for a while. Therefore, sustainable earth, and realization of a civilized society, and the new logic of policy paradigm for a more humane society, should be the focal point for the 21st century and beyond. The Government of the future should continuously create the new possibilities of Smart creativity with the spirit of New Frontier, while wisely and swiftly corresponding to the current turbulent changes of the 4th Industrial Revolutions.

REFERENCES

INTERNATIONAL LITERATURE

Anderson, C. W. (1990). *Pragmatic Liberalism*. Chicago: University of Chicago Press

_____. (1993). Recommending a scheme of reason: political theory, policy science, and democracy. *Policy Science, 26*(3), 215−227.

Ascher, W. (1987). The Evolution of Policy Sciences: Understanding the Rise and Avoiding the fall. *Journal of Policy Analysis and Management, 5*(2), 365−373.

Brunner, R.D. (1991). The Policy Movement as Policy Problem. *Policy Sciences, 24*(1), 65−98.

_____ . (1996). A Milestone in the Policy Sciences. *Policy Sciences, 29*(1), 45−68.

Cobb, R. W., Ross, J. K. and Ross, M. H. (1976). Agenda−Building as a Comparative Political Process, *American Political Science Review, 70*(1), 126−128.

DeLeon, P. (1978). A Theory of Policy Termination. In J. U. May & A. Wildavsky (Eds), *The Policy Cycle*. Beverly Hills: Sage.

_____. (1981). Policy Sciences: The Discipline and the Profession, *Policy Sciences, 1*(13), 1−7.

_____. (1988). *Advice and Consent: The Development of the Policy Sciences*. Russell Sage Foundation.

_____. (1990). Participatory Policy Analysis: Prescriptions and Precautions. *Asian Journal of Public Administration, 12*(1), 29−54.

_____. (1994). Reinventing the Policy Sciences: three steps back to the Future, *Policy Sciences, 27*(1), 77−95.

_____. (1997). *Democracy and The Policy Sciences*. Albany, NY: State University of New York Press.

_____. (1998). Models of Policy Discourse: Insights vs. Prediction. *Policy Studies Journal, 26*(1), 147−161.

_____. (1999). The Stages Approach to the Policy Process: What Has It Done? What Is It Going? In P. Sabatier (Ed), *Theories of the Policy Process*. Boulder, Colorado: Westview Press.

DeLeon, P., & Martell, C. R. (2006). The Policy Sciences: Past, Present, and Future. In G. Peters & J. Pierre (Eds), *Handbook of Public Policy*. London: Sage.

Dror, Y. (1970). Prolegomena to Policy Sciences. *Policy Sciences, 1*(1), 135–150.

_____. (1983). New Advances in Public Policy Teaching. *Journal of Policy Analysis and Management, 2*(3), 449–454.

_____. (1968). *Public Policymaking Reexamined*. San Francisco: Chandler.

Drucker, P. F. (1980). *Managing in Turbulent Times*. New York: Harper and Row.

Dunn, W. (1981) *An Introduce to Public Policy Analysis*. Englewood Cliff: Prentice–Hall.

Dunn, W. (1981). *Public Policy Analysis*. Englewood Cliffs, NJ: Prentice Hall.

Easton, D. (1965), *A Framework for Political Analysis*. Eaglewood Cliff, NJ: Prentice–Hall.

Elmore, R. F. (1985). Forward and Backward Mapping: Reversible Logic in the Analysis of Public Policy, In *Policy Implementation in Federal and Unitary System*.

Etzioni, A. (1964). *Modern organization*. Englewood Cliffs, NJ: Prentice–Hall.

Gourevitch, P. (1978). Second Image Reversed. *International Organization, 32*(4), 881–912.

Habermas, J. (1971). *Knowledge and Human Interests* (J. Shapiro, Trans.). Boston MA: Beacon Press.

_____. (1979). *Communication and the Evolution of Society* (J. Shapiro, Trans.). Boston MA: Beacon Press.

Habermas, J. (1987). *The Philosophical Discourse of Modernity* (F. Lawrence Trans.). Cambridge: MIT Press.

Hall, P. A. (1986). *Governing the Economy: The Politics of State Intervention in Britain and France*. New York: Oxford University Press.

_____. (1996). Political Science and the Three New Institutionalisms. *Political Studies. 44*(5), 936–957.

Heeks, R. (2004). E–Government as a Carrier of Context. *Institute for Development Policy and Management* (No.15).

Ikenberry, G. J. (1988). Conclusion: An Institutional Approach to American Foreign Economic Policy. In G. J. Ikenberry, D. A. Lake, & M. Mastanduno (Eds.), *The State and American Foreign Economic Policy*. Ithaca: Cornell University Press.

Ikenberry, G. J., D. A. Lake, & M. Mastanduno. (1988). Introduction: Approaches to Explaining American Foreign Economic Policy. In G. J. Ikenberry, D. A. Lake, & M. Mastanduno (Eds.), *The State and American Foreign Economic Policy*. Ithaca: Cornell University Press.

Immergut, E. M. (1998). The Theoretical Core of the New Institutionalism. *Politics & Society, 26*(1), 5–34.

Kelly, G., Mulgan, G., & Muers, S. (2002). *Creating Public Value: An Analytical Framework for Public Service Reform*. London: Cabinet Office.

Kelly, T. (1992). *Telecommunications and Broadcasting: Convergence or Collision?* (Vol. 29). Organization for Economic Co–operation and Development. Washington, DC: OECD Publications and Information Centre.

King, G., Keohane. R. O. & Verba, S. (1993). *Designing Social Inquiry*. Princeton: Princeton University Press.

Kingdon, J. W. (1984). *Agendas, Alternatives and Public Policies*. Boston: Little, Brown.

_____. (2003). Modes of Governance. In Kooiman J. (Ed.), *Governing as Governance*. London: Sage.

Krasner, S. D. (1983). Regimes and the Limits of Realism: Regimes as Autonomous Variables. In Krasner (Ed.), *International Regimes*. Ithaca: Cornell University.

Krasner, S. D. (1984). Approaches to the State Alternative Conceptions and Historical Dynamics. *Comparative Politics.* 223–246.

Lasswell, H. D. (1943a), Memorandum: Personal Policy Objectives (October 1). *Archieved at Stering Library*. Yale University, New Haven. CT.

_____. (1943b), Proposal: The Institute of Policy Sciences (October 1). *Archieved at Stering Library*. Yale University, New Haven. CT.

_____. (1949), *Power and Personality*. New York: Norton.

_____. (1955). Current Studies of the Decision Process: Automation versus Creativity. *Western Political Quarterly, 8*(3), 381–399.

_____. (1965a). *World Politics and Personal Insecurity*. New York: The Free Press.

_____. (1965b). The World Revolution of Our Time: A Framework for Basic Policy Research. In H. D. Lasswell & D. Lerner (Eds.), *World Revolutionary Elites: Studies in Coercive Ideological Movements*. Cambridge, MA: The MIT Press.

_____. (1970), The Emerging Conception of the Policy Sciences. *Policy Sciences, 1*(1), 3—14.

_____. (1971). *A Pre—View of Policy Sciences.* New York: Elsevier.

Lasswell, H. D., & Lerner, D. (1951). The policy orientation. *Communication Researchers and Policy-Making.*

Lasswell, H. D., & Macdougal, M. S. (1992). *Jurisprudence of a Free Society. Studies in Law, Science and Policy* (Vol. 2). New Haven, CT: New Haven Press.

Lasswell, H. D., Lerner, D., & Fisher, H. H. (1951). *The policy sciences: Recent Developments in Scope and Method.* Stanford University Press.

Lerner, D. (1975). From Social Science to Policy Science: An Introductory Note. In S. S. Nagel (Ed.), *Policy Studies.* Lexington, Mass: Lexington Books.

Lipsky, M. (1976). Toward a Theory of Street—Level Bureaucracy. In W. D. Hawley, & Michael Lipsky (Eds.), *Theoretical Perspectives on Urban Politics,* Englewoods Cliffs, NJ: Prentice—Hall.

Maslow, A. (1954). *Motivation and Personality,* New York: Harper.

Matland, R. E. (1995). Synthesizing the Implementation Literature: The Ambiguity—Conflict Model of Policy Implementation. *Journal of Public Administration Research and Theory, 5*(2), 145—174.

McLuhan, M. (1964). *Understanding Media.* London: Routledge

Moore, M. H. (1995). *Creating Public Value: Strategic Management in Government.* Harvard University Press.

Osborne, David & P. Plastrik. (1997). *Banishing Bureaucracy: The Five Strategies for Reinventing Government.* Reading. MA: Addision—Wesley.

Ostrom, E. (1986). An Agenda for the Study of Institutions. *Public Choice, 48*(1), 3—25

Ostrom, E. (1990). *Governing the Commons: The Evolution of Institutions for Collective Action.* New York: Cambridge University Press.

Ostrom, E. (1992). *Crafting Institutions for Self—Governing Irrigation Systems.* San Francisco: ICS Press.

Peters G. & Pierre J. (2005). Toward a Theory of Governance. In Peters G. & Pierre J. *Governing Complex Societies: Toward Theory of Governance: New Government—Society Interactions.* Palgrave: Macmillan.

Peters G. (1995). *The Future of Governing.* University Press of Kansas.

Pierre, J. (2000). Introduction: Understanding Governance. In J. Pierre (ed.), *Debating Governance.* Oxford: Oxford University Press.

Pressman, J., & Wildavsky, A. (1973). *Implementation.* Berkely.

Prigogine, I., & Stengers, I. (1984). *Order out of Chaos: Man's New Dialogue with Nature.* New York: Bantam Books.

Putnam, R. (1992). *Making Democracy Work.* Princeton: Princeton University Press.

Putnam, R. (1993). The Prosperous Community: Social Capital and Public Life. *The American Prospect* 13(Spring).

Quinn, Robert E. (1996). *Deep Change: Discovering the Leader Within.* John Wiley & Sons, Inc.

Rhodes R. A. W. (1990). Policy Networks: A British Perspective. *Journal of Theoretical Politics.* 2(3), 293 – 317.

_____. (1997). *Understanding Governance: Policy Networks, Governance: Reflexivity and Accountability.* Open University Press: Buckingham.

_____. (1996). The New Governance: Governing without Government, *Political Studies,* 44(4), 652 – 667.

Rhodes, R., & Marsh D. (1992) New Directions in the Study of Policy Networks. *European Journal of Political Research 21*(1-2), 181 – 205.

Riesman, D. (1966). *The Lonely Crowd.* New York: The Free Press.

Sabatier, P. A. (1986). Top – Down and Bottom – Up Approaches to Implementation Research: A Critical Analysis and Suggested Synthesis. *Journal of Public Policy,* 6(1), 21 – 48.

_____. (1993). Policy Change over a Decade or More. In P. A. Sabatier, & H. C. Jenkins – Smith (Eds.), *Policy Change and Learning.* Boulder, CO: Westview Press.

_____. (1999). *Theories of the Policy Process.* Boulder, CO: Westview.

Sabatier, P. A., & Jenkins – Smith, H. C. (1993). *Policy Change and Learning: An Advocacy Coalition Approach.* Westview Press.

Simon, H. A. (1987). The Steam Engine and Computer: What Makes Technology Revolutionary, *Educom Bulletin,* 22(1), 2 – 5.

Skocpol, T. (1984a). Emerging Agendas and Recurrent Strategies in Historical

Sociology. In T. Skocpol (Ed.), *Vision and Method in Historical Sociology.* Cambridge University Press.

Skocpol, T. (1984b), Sociology's Historical Imagination. In T. Skocpol (Ed.), *Vision and Method in Historical Sociology.* Cambridge University Press.

_____. (1985), Bringing the State Back In: Strategies of Analysis in Current Research. In P. Evans, D. Dietrich, & T. Skocpol (Eds), *Bringing the State Back In.* Cambridge: Cambridge University Press.

Toffler, A. (1970). *Future Schock.* New York: Random Hause.

_____. (1989). *The Third Wave.* Bantam

_____. (1990). *Powershift: Knowledge, Wealth and Violence at the Edge of the 21st Century.* Mass Market Paperback.

Wilson, W. (1887). The Study of Administration, *Political Science Quarterly, 2*(2), 197–222.

Winter, S. (1986). How policy making Affects Implementation: The Decentralization of the Danish Disablement Pension Administration, *Scandinavian Political Studies, 9*(4), 361–385.

_____. (1990). Integrating Implementation Research. In D. J. Palimbo, & D. J. Calista (Eds.), *Implementation and Policy Process,* New York: Greenwood Press.

World Bank. (1998). *Knowledge for Development.* Washington DC: World Bank.

World Economic Forum. (2012). *Future of Government: Fast and Curious.* World Economic Forum.

KOREAN LITERATURE

Jung, Jung Gil. (2000). *New Public Administration.* Seoul: DaeMyung.

Kim, Seok Joon. et al. (2000). *The Study of New Governance.* DaeYoung－Publication Corp.

Kim, Sun Kyung. (2003). The Appearance of U－Government and the Direction of Service, *Digital Administration.* Ministry of Government Administration and Home Affairs.

Kwon, Gi Heon. (2000). The Theoretical Model of Knowledge Government. *Information Society,* 1, 28－47.

Kwon, Gi Heon. (2008). *Theories of Policy Science.* Seoul: Parkyoungsa.

Kwon, Gi Heon. (2010). *Theory of Policy Analysis.* Seoul: Parkyoungsa.

Kwon, Gi Heon. (2014). *E－Government & E－Strategy: Explaining the Successful Korean E－Government Model and Strategies.* Seoul: Parkyoungsa.

Kwon, Gi Heon. (2018). *Theories of Public Administration.* Seoul: Parkyoungsa.

Samsung Economic Research Institute. (1999). *Knowledge Management and the Future of Korea.*

Wilber, Ken. (2016). *Integrative Psychology of Ken Wilber.* Seoul: Hakjisa.

INDEX

the Index of Persons

CURRICULUM VITAE

Gi-Heon Kwon, Ph D

Dean
Graduate School of SKKU

Dean
GePeGi (Global e-Policy & e-Government Institute)

Professor
Graduate School of Governance, SKKU
Public Administration, SKKU

Address
[Research Room] Law School B/D Room 320
                 SKKU(SungKyunKwan Univ.)
                 53 Myung Ryun Dong 3-Ga, Jong Rho-Gu,
                 Seoul P.O.BOX 110-745

[E-mail] gkwon77@empas.com
[TEL]   +82-2-760-0363(office)

ACADEMIC BACKGROUNDS

- 1991-1994   Ph. D in Public Policy,
  Graduate School of Arts & Science, Harvard University

- 1989-1991   Masters in Public Policy (MPP),
  John F. Kennedy School of Government, Harvard University

- 1983-1985   Masters in Public Administration (MPA),
  Graduate School of Public Administration, Seoul National University

- 1979-1983   Bachelor's Degree in Public Administration (BA),
  Han Kook University of Foreign Studies

AWARDS

- Prime Minister's Award
  (Ranked Top among the 26th Senior Government Entrance Exam)
- Fulbright Scholarship
- Best Thesis Award, APPAM
  (America Public Policy Analysis & Management Association)
- Best Thesis Award, Korea Association for Public Administration
- Academic Scholarship, MPP & Ph.D. in Public Policy, Harvard University
- Fulbright Visiting Scholar, Maxwell School, Syracuse University, USA
  (Lecture: e-Government/National Innovation)
- Best Book Award (two times), Korea National Academy of Science
- Best Book Award, Ministry of Culture & Tourism
- Passed the 26th Senior Government Entrance Exam (1982)

ACADEMIC ACTIVITIES

- 2015-2016   President
               Korean Association for Policy Studies

- 2009-2010   Editor in Chief,
               Korean Association for Policy Studies

- 2008   Chairman,
               Special Research Committee, Korean Association for Policy Studies

- 2005-2007   Editorial Committee,
               Korean Association for Policy Studies

- 2005   Chairman,
               Academic Information Committee, Korea Association for Public
               Administration

- 2004   Chairman,
               Special Policy Case Committee, Korean Association for Policy Studies

- 2003-2005   Editorial Committee,
               Korean Association for Public Administration

PUBLICATIONS

Monographs

- 2021   Reflection on Policy Science
- 2020   Life After COVID-19 Crisis
- 2019   Wisdom of Policy Science
- 2018   Concert of Policy Science

              Feast of Policy Science
- 2017   Government 4.0
- 2014   E-Government and E-Strategies:

              Explaining Successful Conditions of Korean e-Government
- 2014   Lectures on Public Administration
- 2014   Lectures on Policy Science
- 2014   How to Reform Public Enterprises?
- 2013   Electronic Government
- 2013   What is the Justice of the Nation?

              Concert of Public Administration
- 2010   Theories of Policy Analysis
- 2009   Theories of Public Administration
- 2008   Theories of Future Foresight
- 2008   The Logic of Public Policy
- 2008   Theories of Public Policy
- 2004   Public Management Information System

Teaching/Consulting/Research Areas

- e-Government & e-Policy
- Smart Governance
- Policy Analysis
- Theories on Policy Science
- National Innovation
- Policy Foresight
- Policy Making

POLICY SCIENCE: Effective Policy Making under the Age of Turbulence

Printed the first edition in 2021. 4. 16
Published the first edition in 2021. 4. 30

Author	Gi-Heon Kwon
President	Jong-Man An · Sang-Joon An
Publishing Company	Parkyoung Publishing & Company
	#210, 53, Gasan digital 2-ro, Geumcheon-gu, Seoul
	Registered in 1959.3.11. 300-1959-1

tel	82-2-733-6771
fax	82-2-736-4818
e-mail	pys@pybook.co.kr
homepage	www.pybook.co.kr

ISBN 979-11-303-1201-9 93350

23,000 ₩ (Korean Currency)